Praise for
Hacking the Human Mind

"Superb marketing is both an art and a science. I know of no better proof than in the engaging and illuminating content of this book, which shows how some of our most successful brands simultaneously mastered each to great effect."

— **Robert Cialdini,** *New York Times* **bestselling author,** *Influence* **and** *Pre-Suasion*

"This is a great book. Practical, generous and insightful."

— **Seth Godin, 22-time bestselling author, entrepreneur and teacher**

"This is a book for the ages. The authors have ingeniously used behavioral science to reverse-engineer the psychological genius that lies hidden behind many of the world's greatest brands."

— **Rory Sutherland, Vice Chairman at Ogilvy, UK, and author,** *Alchemy*

"A fascinating look at how today's top brands have used subtle cues and smart design to draw attention and inspire action. Wonderful mix of rigorous evidence and quirky stories, told in a way that's clear, practical, and fun to read. Ideas and tactics you can put to work immediately."

— **Jonah Berger, Professor and bestselling author,** *Contagious* **and** *The Catalyst*

"You'll discover behavioral science through the world's most iconic brands, and you'll get insight into those brands' practices through the basic principles of behavioral science. Shotton and Flicker have crafted a smart, witty, and incredibly useful guide for anyone looking to understand (and influence) humans."

— **Ayelet Fishbach, Professor and author,** *Get It Done*

"If you want to change human behaviour, you need to understand human behaviour. Read this book and you're off to a flying start. Behavioural science distilled into simple, easy-to-apply 'mind hacks', not just to retrospectively explain other brands' successes, but to help us all proactively plan for *our* brand's success."

— **Sarah Carter, Global Planning Partner at adam&eveDDB and co-author,** *How Not To Plan*

"If you like your creative inspiration backed up by hard numbers and provable statistics, instead of just empty rhetoric, this is the book for you."

— **Dave Trott, Creative director and author,** *Predatory Thinking*

"Part storytelling, part practical insight, all valuable. *Hacking the Human Mind* is a must read for every marketer. Enjoy the fun and fascinating stories from your favorite brands, with details of the science-backed reasons behind their success so you can see some of your own. Do yourself a favor and pick up this book before your competition does."

— **Melina Palmer, CEO, The Brainy Business and author,** *The Truth About Pricing*

"Shotton and Flicker blend vivid storytelling with cutting-edge research to explain how subtle cues, framing, and behavioral biases influence everyday decisions. Whether you're a marketer, entrepreneur, or just fascinated by what makes people tick, this is your essential guide to turning insight into impact."

— **Tali Sharot, Professor and author,** *The Influential Mind*

HACKING
THE
HUMAN
MIND

HACKING THE HUMAN MIND

THE BEHAVIORAL SCIENCE SECRETS BEHIND 17 OF THE WORLD'S BEST BRANDS

RICHARD SHOTTON
MICHAELAARON FLICKER

HARRIMAN HOUSE LTD
Website: harriman.house

First published in 2025 by Harriman House, an imprint of Pan Macmillan
Associated companies throughout the world
www.panmacmillan.com

Copyright © Richard Shotton and MichaelAaron Flicker 2025

The rights of Richard Shotton and MichaelAaron Flicker to be identified as the authors have been asserted in accordance with the Copyright, Design and Patents Act 1988.

Paperback ISBN: 978-1-80409-132-6
eBook ISBN: 978-1-80409-133-3

All rights reserved. No part of this publication may be reproduced, stored in a retrieval system, or transmitted in any form or by any means (including without limitation electronic, mechanical, photocopying, recording, or otherwise) without the prior written permission of the publisher. This book is sold subject to the condition that it shall not, by way of trade or otherwise, be lent, hired out, or otherwise circulated without the publisher's prior consent. This work is reserved from text and data mining (Article 4(3) Directive (EU) 2019/790).

Harriman House does not have any control over, or any responsibility for, any author or third-party websites (including without limitation URLs, emails and QR codes) referred to in or on this book. This book is for informational purposes only. Readers are advised to consult an appropriate professional in light of their relevant circumstances and requirements before acting on any information in this book.

No responsibility or liability for loss occasioned to any person or corporate body acting or refraining to act as a result of reading material in this book can be accepted by the publisher, by the authors, or by the employers of the authors.

01

Printed in the United States of America.

Cover design by Christopher Parker.

CONTENTS

Introduction: Five Guys ... 1
   Goal dilution effect ... 2

Chapter 1: Kraft Mac & Cheese ... 7
   Expectation assimilation ... 9
   Pareidolia ... 16

Chapter 2: Starbucks' Pumpkin Spice Latte ... 21
   Scarcity ... 23
   Nostalgia ... 26

Chapter 3: Snickers ... 29
   Trigger moments ... 31
   Humor ... 34

Chapter 4: Apple ... 41
   Concreteness ... 43
   Optimal newness ... 49

Chapter 5: Amazon Prime ... 53
   Sunk cost fallacy ... 55
   Charm pricing ... 61

Chapter 6: Aperol — 65
- Social proof — 67
- Averted gaze — 72

Chapter 7: Häagen-Dazs — 75
- Foreign branding — 77
- Descriptive language — 81

Chapter 8: Red Bull — 87
- Price relativity — 88
- Price as a badge of quality — 93
- Costly signaling — 94

Chapter 9: Guinness — 99
- Pratfall effect — 102

Chapter 10: Liquid Death — 109
- Von Restorff effect — 111
- Red sneakers effect — 113
- Mere exposure effect — 116

Chapter 11: Dyson — 123
- Illusion of effort — 125
- Danger of claimed data — 132

Chapter 12: Facebook — 135
- Uncertain rewards — 137
- Make it easy — 144

CONTENTS

Chapter 13: Klarna — 147
- Present bias — 149
- Temporal reframing — 151

Chapter 14: Got Milk? — 155
- Loss aversion — 158
- Messenger effect — 161

Chapter 15: Kentucky Fried Chicken — 165
- Information gaps — 167
- Zeigarnik effect — 170
- False scarcity — 172

Chapter 16: Pringles — 177
- Keats heuristic — 179
- Synesthesia — 182

Conclusion — 187
- Semmelweis reflex — 189

Further Resources — 193

References — 197

Endnotes — 207

Acknowledgments — 211

About the Authors — 213

INTRODUCTION: FIVE GUYS

IMAGINE A SUNNY day on the boardwalk in Ocean City, Maryland. It's the mid-1980s, muscle tees and acid-washed denim abound. Jerry Murrell is out with his four almost-adult sons.

Jerry had offered his oldest boys a choice: go to college if they desired, or use the funds to start a business. They opted for the latter. So getting the family enterprise off the ground mattered — in fact, their futures depended on it. They were always on the lookout for inspiration.

And on that day, amid the garish food shacks, Jerry and his sons were struck by one seller in particular: Thrasher's French Fries. Because Thrasher's offered one thing: fries, nothing more. Just great fries. Jerry was struck by the simplicity of it:

> I saw something I just couldn't believe... they had a place selling boardwalk fries... There must've been 20 places selling boardwalk fries, but only one place had a long line. And that was Thrasher's. The line was 100ft long all day long.
> So me and the kids, that got into our minds... Hamburgers. Fries. Keep it simple. Might work. And that's where the idea came from.[1]

In 1986, Arlington, VA, Jerry and his family opened the first Five Guys Burgers and Fries.

Five Guys prides itself on offering the best burger and fries. When they first opened, there was no vegan or fish option, no chicken, no salads, no ice cream. The focus was squarely on high-quality beef patties served with a generous portion of top-notch fries.

Jerry thought it might work, and it did. The first store thrived, Jerry quit his day job and in 2002, as the brand grew, they began offering franchises. Since then, Five Guys has grown to become one of America's favorites in the "better burger" category, and is taking off globally with over 1,800 stores worldwide, and 1,500 more on the way.[2]

Doing one thing beautifully

Murrell clearly had a nose for business. Because he sniffed out the major reason for Thrasher's success — an aspect with a strong behavioral science foundation.

In choosing to focus on only one product, he was applying a finding from psychology called the *goal dilution effect*. It's fascinating and somewhat counterintuitive: people tend to believe a product or service is less effective when it claims to achieve many things, compared to when it focuses on a single purpose.

People tend to believe a product or service is less effective when it claims to achieve many things, compared to when it focuses on a single purpose.

A key study revealing this psychological phenomenon was carried out in 2007 by Ying Zhang and Ayelet Fishbach at the University of Chicago. They gave people information describing how eating tomatoes could achieve either one goal ("help prevent cancer"), or two goals ("help prevent cancer and degenerative disease of the eye"). Participants were then asked to rate how effective eating tomatoes was at achieving the first goal (preventing cancer).

Strangely, people rated eating tomatoes as *12% more effective* at preventing cancer when this was given as the *only* benefit, compared to being listed along with another goal. It's not logical. But we are more confident when just one advantage is presented.

The goal dilution effect has a clear implication for any marketer — focus on conveying one clear benefit to your customers. If you add multiple reasons to believe, it will dilute the credibility and impact of the core reason.

This phenomenon seems to be one that Murrell was intuitively alert to. The Five Guys menu is much shorter than your average burger joint. This primes customers to expect that the food will be delicious. In effect, the exact same burger will be rated as tastier than it would if served by an all-purpose chain. Of course — Five Guys still has to be a great brand, with great service and a great product. But the goal dilution effect gives them an edge.

They now serve 165 million burgers a year.[3] Those Five Guys (now, the five Murrell sons) are raking in over $2.3 billion in sales per year.[4]

And all made a little more possible because Murrell picked an evidence-based behavioral insight from a brand he admired.

Why this story matters

We — like Murrell — believe that one of the surest ways to get better, faster, is to learn from others. That's what this book is all about.

But most brands are more complex than Thrasher's Fries. It's hard to tease out what's responsible for their success when they apply hundreds of marketing moves simultaneously.

In this book, we analyze some of the world's most successful companies through the lens of behavioral science. Of all the tactics they have used, we highlight the ones that have been proven to work in controlled conditions.

Chapter by chapter, we take each brand in turn — looking at the principles they used, the behavioral science that backs them up, and the practical takeaways any marketer can use.

Identifying those tactics that have a solid behavioral science underpinning will help you decide which aspects of a brand you might want to adopt for yourself — so you can get rid of the guesswork and power up your own efforts with evidence.

This isn't imitation — it's a shortcut. A way to leap years ahead of expensive trial and error by learning what others have already figured out.

Evidence: there for the taking

This book is not just about "what worked" — it's about *why*. We connect the dots between marketing success and the behavioral science that explains it.

What do we mean by behavioral science?

It combines ideas from psychology, sociology, economics, and neuroscience, aiming to uncover human biases through scientific research. Essentially, it's a collection of peer-reviewed, academic experiments that reveal how people actually behave. Not how they claim to, or as logic might suggest they should.

> "Thinking is to humans as swimming is to cats: they can do it, but they'd prefer not to."
> — Daniel Kahneman

There's a broad idea that humans don't like to expend too much energy in order to reach a decision. It's been succinctly summed up by psychologist Susan Fiske, who described people as "cognitive misers." Or, as Daniel Kahneman wittily put it: "Thinking is to humans as swimming is to cats: they can do it, but they'd prefer not to."

Instead, the human brain takes shortcuts, using quick rules of thumb that are often hard-wired, subconscious processes. And these are prone to systematic errors, or what we call behavioral biases. Crucially, if you're aware of these biases you can work with human nature, rather than against it. And that will always be more effective.

Around the world, researchers are running randomized controlled trials, testing interventions, and publishing papers that show how humans actually make decisions. But their findings are rarely put to commercial use.

We think that needs to change. As businesses, we've relied too long on instinct, intuition, "marketing magic," and not enough on evidence.

That's what brought the two of us together — Richard from London, MichaelAaron from New York — both searching for better ways to make marketing more effective. Different countries, same problem: **how do we make sure the money we spend is actually changing people's behavior?**

We created a podcast, "Behavioral Science for Brands", to explore these topics and decided to write this book to share some of our biggest learnings thus far.

How this book works

Each chapter focuses on a single leading brand, opening with the story of its success and dissecting some of its winning elements. We go beneath the surface to connect their actions to behavioral science principles.

This isn't just about theory. It's about making clear

recommendations for marketers, agencies, and anyone who runs a brand.

So we close each chapter with three key takeaways. These are brief summaries of the main behavioral insights, giving you an at-a-glance reminder of how to take action. Simple tools that you can use in your next brief, your next pitch, or your next board meeting.

Our hope is that you move beyond treating these chapters as interesting case studies. That you take the insights seriously enough to try them. Test them. And make your brand work better by aligning it more closely with how people actually behave.

We're doing that with clients, with students, and with our own portfolio of brands. And we hope you'll do the same.

1

KRAFT MAC & CHEESE

Mmm, mac and cheese. The ultimate quick and easy comfort food. All creamy carbs and melty cheese — and we're under no illusion that it's any kind of healthy.

But its nutritional credentials may be better than you think. And Kraft was, well, a bit crafty, when it came to making some health-focused improvements to its popular convenience food.

Let's take a look at what worked so well for this brand.

A hint of Italian

Macaroni and cheese has European roots, although it's not as entirely Italian as you might expect for a pasta dish. A 14th-century English cookbook featured a dish called makerouns made of pasta and cheese — described at the time as pieces of boiled dough layered with cheese and butter.

So, in one form or another, Europeans have been enjoying the dish for at least 600 years.

It took a while longer for the recipe to cross the Atlantic: the story goes that the personal chef to Thomas Jefferson was so impressed with the dish on a visit to Paris that he brought it back for his boss.

Early versions of mac and cheese were high effort, involving making pasta from scratch and whipping up a cheesy accompaniment. The concept of a convenient pasta and cheese combination didn't arrive until the 1920s, when a salesman struck on the idea of attaching packs of Kraft cheese to boxes of pasta with a rubber band and selling them as a pair.

Kraft developed the idea and in 1937, just before the outbreak of World War II, the brand sold its first boxed macaroni and cheese. It was an immediate hit. Wartime dairy and meat rationing had a lot to do with this success: shoppers could get hold of two Kraft Dinners for just one coupon, helping stretched households to feed the family. Another important factor was that, with more women working away from home during the war, convenience foods were taking off. And, of course, you didn't need a fridge to store it.*

In the first year of launch alone, nine million boxes were sold.[5] And its popularity hasn't dipped since: Kraft now reportedly sells one million boxes per day.[6]

How we process processed foods

Given the ever-growing emphasis on the need for more natural foods, you might expect enthusiasm for highly processed Kraft Dinners to be waning.

Seeing the way the nutritional wind was blowing, Kraft decided it was time to improve the health credentials of its recipe, and cut out artificial ingredients like preservatives, flavorings and

---

* Fridges weren't commonplace in US homes until the end of the 1940s.

colorings. But, counter to what many brands might do, it kept quiet about the move.

In 2016, the ingredients list changed. For example, instead of the artificial colorings that previously lent the dish its dayglow orange hue, we saw instead a selection of natural spices: paprika, turmeric and annatto.

And guess what? Nobody seemed to notice. Or, if they noticed, they didn't mind. Sales remained strong — Kraft had successfully healthified one of its leading products by stealth.

Why didn't they trumpet the recipe improvements? Well, it's possible the brand knew about an important behavioral bias we call *expectation assimilation*.

We taste what we expect to taste

The expectation assimilation phenomenon defines how, in general, we get what we expect to get. Our experiences are significantly influenced by our expectations.

Unfortunately for healthier brands, we expect foods that are good for us to taste bad. Perhaps we recall being urged to eat bland veggies as a child. Or perhaps it's the strong evolutionary advantage to being naturally drawn to sweet, high-fat, calorie-dense foods. Either way, in our minds, healthy = yuk.

Now, as rational adults, we know that nutritious food can also be tasty. But somehow, we still expect an unpleasant experience. And this negative expectation can become self-fulfilling.

One study looking at this was conducted in 2006 by Rajagopal Raghunathan of UT Austin's McCombs School of Business, and colleagues. They gave guests at a party an Indian yogurt drink called a mango lassi.

It wasn't a particularly well-known drink, allowing researchers to explore initial reactions to the new experience. Half of the guests were told the lassi was healthy; the other half that it was unhealthy. All were asked to rate whether they liked it.

The results were revealing. Those who believed the drink to be unhealthy rated it as 55% tastier than those who thought it was good for them. The very idea of healthiness negatively impacted taste perception.

There's more research showing we prefer the experience of something we know (or believe) to be a little bit naughty.

And it's not just our perception of flavor that's influenced by what we expect — it's our behavior as well. Evidence of this comes from a 2017 study by Bradley Turnwald and colleagues from Stanford University, who explored the effect of descriptions on food consumption.

In a large university cafeteria, they randomized the descriptions of vegetable dishes on offer. Each day for seven weeks, a chosen plant-based dish was randomly labeled in one of four ways:

- basic (e.g., "plant-based beans and shallots");
- healthy restrictive (e.g., "light 'n' low-carb plant-based beans and shallots");
- healthy positive (e.g., "healthy energy-boosting plant-based beans and shallots"); and
- indulgent (e.g., "sweet sizzlin' plant-based beans and crispy shallots").

In alignment with the lassi study, labeling dishes as healthy had unfortunate consequences. A healthy description made it less likely that people would pick vegetables. In fact, *healthy positive* labels reduced sales by 7% and *healthy restrictive* by 11% compared to the basic option.

The most effective way of boosting vegetable consumption was to describe the dishes in an *indulgent* way — that increased sales by 25% versus the basic option.

Chart 1: Indulgent labels increase sales more than healthy ones

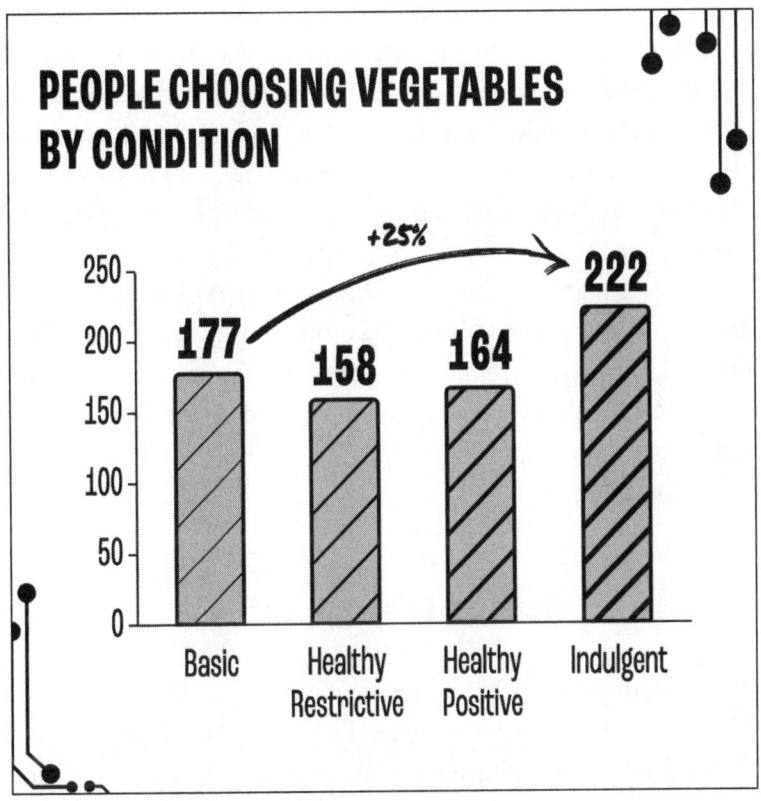

Source: Adapted from Turnwald (2017).

So, the exact same dish was purchased significantly more often when described in tasty terms rather than healthy. This finding has widespread applications. When marketers are trying to encourage behaviors that have an ethical purpose — for example, sustainable or healthy products — they normally default to stressing that virtuous element. However, the Turnwald study suggests a more counter-intuitive approach. Sometimes the best way to promote the most wholesome of products is to focus on appeal, not duty.

If that sounds a little abstract, consider Tesla. When they launched, they focused on desirability not environmental benefits — they emphasized the car as a status symbol with out-of-this-world acceleration rather than promoting its low carbon emissions.

Or consider Budweiser's original non-alcoholic offering. Rather than just emphasize what people were missing out on, they called it Prohibition Brew. A tantalising way of adding some mystique to the product.

It seems that Kraft knew the risks of emphasizing healthiness. Initially, there was no flagging of the new product's healthier credentials. Kraft's genius was waiting until everyone had been eating the dish for several months before highlighting the ingredient change. And those few months were a crucial part of its campaign.

Timing is everything

Kraft's strategy was based on holding back.

In fact, it based an entire campaign around the delayed reveal of the recipe changes. Going public after three months, it admitted that customers had been buying the new product without knowing it.

With 50 million boxes sold during that time, Kraft called this the "World's Biggest Blind Taste Test."[7] On the day of the big reveal, ads featured headlines like, "We would invite you to try it, but you already have" and the social hashtag #didntnotice.

The resulting media traction was impressive, and strong sales followed.

There is experimental evidence to suggest this approach is likely to be effective. Getting customers to try a product before announcing a possible negative change removes the opportunity for expectation assimilation to kick in.

In 2006, Leonard Lee from Columbia University, alongside

colleagues, conducted a study into how people's expectations influence their preferences. They asked 388 bar-goers to taste two drinks: a regular beer (Budweiser) and one called "MIT brew" (the regular beer plus a few drops of balsamic vinegar).

Drinkers were split into three groups. The first group tasted the beers without knowing about the secret ingredient (the vinegar). When questioned, 59% of them preferred the MIT brew.

The second group were told that the MIT brew contained vinegar before tasting. Consistent with the other experiments we've discussed, hearing about an off-putting ingredient affected taste perceptions. In this setup, a mere 30% favored the MIT brew.

The third group were told that the beer contained vinegar too — but only *after* tasting (and before indicating their preferences). Here, 52% of drinkers preferred the MIT brew. That's almost double compared to those told about the vinegar *before* sampling.

Table 1: Telling people about an unappealing ingredient after sampling worked best

	PERCENTAGE PREFERRING MIT BREW
Not told about vinegar in MIT brew	59%
Told about vinegar **before** drinking	30%
Told about vinegar **after** drinking	52%

+73%

Source: Adapted from Lee (2006).

Participants who know about the vinegar before drinking are presumably imagining they can taste it when they take a sip. When told about it after tasting, they can't retrospectively change their initial reaction.

The implication is clear: if you have to reveal information that could create negative taste perceptions, do so *after* your customers have had a chance to sample the product. Once people have come to their own conclusions about a taste, the influence of expectation assimilation is weakened.

Kraft knew this and gave their customers plenty of time to experience the new recipe before revealing changes that risked negatively impacting perceived flavor.

There are plenty of simple ways you can apply these findings. Say you're launching a healthier variant of your brand, perhaps a reduced-sugar soda or fat-free chips. If you run a sampling program, before you give customers the product, make sure to set positive expectations by focusing on the taste credentials. Only afterwards should you mention the lack of sugar or fat.

'Future you' will love it

Of course, some brands just have to talk about healthy benefits upfront. If this is you, behavioral science offers another useful insight.

The most effective approach is likely to involve targeting customers who are making decisions for the future. Because there's evidence to show that we're pretty bad at predicting what our future selves will want.

In 1998, Daniel Read and Barbara van Leeuwen from Leeds University ran a study looking at how timing impacts food decisions. Two hundred employees in Denmark were assigned to one of two groups:

- Group one were offered either an apple or a candy bar that they would receive in one week.
- Group two were offered either an apple or a candy bar to eat straight away.

Around 50% of participants in group one chose the apple, knowing they would receive the snack in a week's time. However, for group two, who received the snack right away, only 19% went for the healthier apple — 81% instead opted for candy. So, half the participants chose the apple for their future selves, even though the evidence suggests that candy would be better appreciated at the point of consumption.

Table 2: Choices for the future self vary from current preferences

	APPLE	CANDY BAR
Eat in one week	50%	50%
Eat immediately	19%	81%

Source: Adapted from Read and van Leeuwen (1998).

If you've ever found yourself having to pre-order for a group dinner, this same bias may have swayed you. Did you pick the healthy fish option with steamed vegetables and baked potatoes and then stare ruefully at your fellow diners' steak and fries?

What this means for brands is that if you're selling something that customers think they *should* want, focus your efforts on well-planned purchasing situations, such as the weekly online grocery shop.

In contrast, candy bars and other indulgences are best marketed as last-minute, unplanned treats at the checkout. Which is exactly why you'll find them there.

Serve with a smile

So, Kraft has effectively managed the issue of expectation assimilation in order to introduce healthy changes without inciting a revolt among fans.

But this is not the only marketing wizardry at play. Kraft also harnesses a fascinating bias called *pareidolia*. Have you ever spotted a face in an unlikely place? On the headlights of a passing car? Or a church door, like the image below? That's pareidolia.

Figure 1: St. Nicholas Church in Tallinn

Source: Shotton (2024).

CHAPTER 1: KRAFT MAC & CHEESE

Humans are hardwired to pick out patterns — and particularly faces — from randomness. We see recognizable things in clouds, marks on the wall, burnt bits of toast, etc.; and the phenomenon lies at the heart of the psychological assessment called the Rorschach inkblot test.

Pareidolia has long been recognized as a human trait. Leonardo da Vinci reportedly once said:

> If you look at any walls spotted with various stains or with a mixture of different kinds of stones, if you are about to invent some scene you will be able to see in it a resemblance to various different landscapes adorned with mountains, rivers, rocks, trees, plains, wide valleys, and various groups of hills.

As with many — if not all — of the biases we discuss, the explanation may be evolutionary. As a species, we would never have survived without other people to help us. We're tribal. So, a powerful ability to recognize faces has been fundamental to our existence.

As David Robson put it in a 2014 article on the subject:

> Human survival depends so heavily on others — whether we need their help, or fear their violence — that we need to react quickly and understand their motives. So the brain may be wired to quickly detect others whenever it can. If we occasionally make a mistake and see a face in tree bark, that's less serious than failing to spot someone hiding in the bushes.

There's evidence from psychology to show that this is still an influential bias. Gianluigi Guido at the University of Salento led a study that showed that facelike objects were particularly likely to grab our attention.

In 2019, the researchers showed 154 participants pairs of print ads, one with a pareidolian face and one without.

They found that in 80% of ad pairs, the one with a pareidolian face received significantly greater attention than its faceless counterpart. Interestingly, this attention-grabbing capacity was most effective during the shortest exposure to ads (0.5 seconds), where 92% of the pareidolian versions received the greatest attention.

Kraft has successfully exploited the pareidolian phenomenon with its packaging, which features a macaroni smile. And it's turned that noodle smile into one of its biggest brand assets. All of which helps to grab attention in the supermarket — and encourage shoppers to indulge in some comfort eating (without artificial ingredients).

> "If your advertising goes unnoticed, everything else is academic."
> — Bill Bernbach

So, the final learning that marketers can take from Kraft is a simple design one: don't underestimate the power of pareidolia. If you can add a design element to your packaging or ads that bears even a passing resemblance to a face, you'll be more likely to catch people's attention. According to Guido's study this is especially important in settings with limited dwell time, like a store or online.

And attention is not just a nice-to-have; it's an essential ingredient of a successful campaign. As the creative director Bill Bernbach said, "If your advertising goes unnoticed, everything else is academic."

CHAPTER 1: KRAFT MAC & CHEESE

THREE KEY TAKEAWAYS

1. **Don't lead with the lettuce**: Customers equate healthiness with bad taste. Unfortunately, those expectations become self-fulfilling and affect the actual experience of the product. So, think carefully before you focus on goodness.

2. **Time your health pitch right**: If your healthy credentials are a critical message, target customers who are planning for the future. When we're thinking about our future selves, we're much more likely to behave in the way we feel we *ought* to. That's when a health message resonates best.

3. **Put a face to it**: Don't underestimate the power of a face. Customers are instinctively drawn to them.

2

STARBUCKS' PUMPKIN SPICE LATTE

Nothing heralds the shift from summer to fall quite like the annual release of Starbucks' Pumpkin Spice Latte. So iconic that it now has its own Wikipedia page, merchandise and fan clubs, the beverage has been one of the coffee giant's most popular since its launch in 2003.

So, what lies at the heart of this sweet success? A few standout behavioral biases have lent a hand.

A seafaring past

There's something a little fishy about the Starbucks logo, with its mermaid-esque figure. In fact, while there's nothing particularly mythical about the brand heritage, there is an oceanic link.

The name was inspired by a combination of a *Moby Dick* character, first mate Starbuck, and a town on an 1800s map: Starbos. The brand team had been searching for something starting with a

St, believing this to be a powerful sound — and they were right, in this case.

According to Gordon Bowker, one of the original co-founders, it's the sound of the word more than any link to the ocean that matters — although the website has a more lyrical claim that the name "evoked the romance of the high seas and the seafaring tradition of the early coffee traders."

Bowker and colleagues established the flagship Starbucks store in Seattle in 1971, originally to sell roasted coffee beans and coffee-making kit. It wasn't until the 1980s that new owner Howard Schultz took Starbucks in the cafe direction. He'd founded a coffeehouse brand called Il Giornale, inspired by a trip to Italy, where he saw customers relaxing and socializing over their espressos. In an attempt to capture this continental style, his establishments featured opera music on loop, baristas in bowties and global newspapers to read.

So when the Il Giornale chain acquired Starbucks, a similar, if less flamboyant, vibe took over. Soon new stores opened up and coffeehouse culture had arrived in the US. Some Italian influences remained — a focus on top-quality espresso-based drinks, as well as the coffee vernacular that we now know so well. Other ideas, like the opera music, were dropped — perhaps wisely.

Forty years on and Starbucks is the world's biggest coffeehouse chain, with more than 35,000 stores in 80 countries.[8]

Seasonal favorites

Starbucks stores serve up an everchanging menu of drinks, many of which have little in common with a classic Italian espresso — how about a lavender crème frappuccino for Spring?

But there are some favorites that return year after year, including the Pumpkin Spice Latte (PSL). Described as an "espresso combined with pumpkin flavor sauce, topped with a blend of cinnamon, ginger, nutmeg, and cloves," it's top of the beverage list for millions of Starbucks fans. In its first ten years of sales, Starbucks sold over 200 million Pumpkin Spice Lattes.[9]

For many, the PSL signals the change of season, ushering in darker evenings and time spent snuggled up cozily with a steaming mug in your hands.

Much has been written about the marketing genius that is the Pumpkin Spice Latte — but what's going on from a behavioral science perspective?

For a limited time only

A major key to the success of the PSL is its seasonality: you can only purchase the drink within a specific window each year, between September and November.

This is the first clever application of behavioral science. Because psychology tells us that we want what we can't have. As soon as the question of a limit arises, our desire for the scarce resource peaks.

Research sheds light on this and suggests what's happening in our minds. One interesting study was conducted in 2010 by Suzanne Shu at the Anderson School of Management, UCLA and Ayelet Gneezy at the University of California in San Diego.

The researchers offered participants a gift voucher worth $6 for a free coffee and cake at a local cafe. They randomly gave participants one of two different vouchers, one expiring in three weeks and the other in two months.

You might expect that the longer window would give customers a better chance to spend their vouchers. But the results showed the opposite: when the expiry date was two months away, only 6% of vouchers were redeemed; but with a short deadline of just three weeks, 33% of vouchers were used.

The researchers hypothesized that the small window for action removed any opportunity to procrastinate. Customers realized that if they didn't use the voucher soon, they would lose out.

Something similar is going on with the Pumpkin Spice Latte. If you don't go out and buy the drink when it's released, you know you won't be able to for the rest of the year. If you like it, you have to buy it right away.

So, you've enjoyed your PSL between September and November. After that, you're forced to take a break — and it seems that stepping away from the drink for a while also boosts its desirability.

That holiday feeling

Much of the pleasure of the special moments in our lives lies in the joy of anticipation.

Research by Tali Sharot, a professor of cognitive neuroscience at University College London, revealed the factors that fuel that happy "holiday feeling": the initial sense of anticipation, plus a whole series of "firsts" — things like your first glimpse of the hotel, your first cocktail, your first dip in the pool. Sharot explained that these "firsts" are important because novelty is rewarding in itself. It gives our brains a spark of positivity. If Pumpkin Spice Lattes were on offer year-round, customers wouldn't enjoy the pleasure of anticipation or the buzz that accompanies that first sip in September.

As well as delivering anticipation and the annual joy of the first taste, the break in availability from November to September is important for another reason.

Because it turns out that one way to boost joy is simply to interrupt it. New York University's Leif D. Nelson and Tom Meyvis explored this surprising phenomenon in a 2008 study.

The researchers recruited participants who were told they would be reviewing a massage cushion. Participants were split into two groups. The first group used the device for three minutes (180 seconds) without interruption. The second group used the massage cushion for two periods of 80 seconds, with a 20-second break between sessions. Afterwards, participants were asked to rate their enjoyment of the massage on a nine-point scale (one = not pleasant; nine = extremely pleasant).

Those who had a three-minute massage gave an average rating of 6.05 out of 9. However, those forced to take a 20-second break during their massage gave a rating of 7.05 — that's a 17% improvement in satisfaction.

At first glance, that's counter-intuitive. The group who had the shorter massage enjoyed it more. But the theory is that the break in pleasure prevents us from becoming too familiar with the positive experience and thus noticing it less — a process called *habituation*.

Studies like this suggest that if Pumpkin Spice Lattes were available year-round, we'd quickly become habituated to them and our appreciation of the treat would decline.

It can be extremely tempting for a brand to cash in on popularity and extend to permanent availability. But this can backfire. In the 1980s, there was an attempt in the UK to relax the limited shelf time for Cadbury's Creme Eggs. Previously only available in the run-up to Easter, the treats were trialed in stores year-round. This resulted in a slide in sales as the novelty wore off. The brand quickly reverted to seasonal availability.

> **The break in pleasure prevents us from becoming too familiar with the positive experience and thus noticing it less.**

This idea isn't just relevant to food and drink. Disney were once the masters of applying this concept. In the 1980s when the video market was booming they came up with the "Disney Vault." They never made all their animated titles available at any one time. Instead they would release a film for a limited period and then remove it from sale — or in their lingo, "put the titles back in the vault."

The films stayed off sale for up to a decade. This approach allowed them to create hype around the launch and then, in the run-up to the removal of the items from sale, stress the urgency of buying now.

Or on a much smaller scale, consider retailers like Bath and Body Works. They release seasonal scents, like Winter Candy Apple, for a brief window each year.

Think about your product range. Could you add some seasonal specials? Or could you revitalize an old favorite by removing it from sale for a few months? Paradoxically, sometimes restricting sales can be the best way to boost them.

Happy memories

And there's another crucial behavioral factor working in favor of the Pumpkin Spice Latte. Because if it wasn't also such a desirable item, nobody would be moved to buy it, however limited the purchase window. So, why do we love it so much?

It's more than how it tastes; it's about how it makes us feel. Here, Starbucks is tapping into one more mental trick: the power of *nostalgia*.

It makes intuitive sense, but there's also scientific evidence that nostalgia impacts purchasing behavior. In 2014, Jannine Lasaleta at the Grenoble School of Management, alongside colleagues, carried out one such study.

They asked participants to look at one of two print ads. The first was designed to elicit a general sense of nostalgia, encouraging readers to recall a special memory from their own past. The second talked about special moments yet to happen.

CHAPTER 2: STARBUCKS' PUMPKIN SPICE LATTE

In the next part of the experiment, researchers showed participants a booklet of 24 product options and asked them to indicate how much they would pay for each.

The products ranged from high-value (e.g., a motorcycle) to midrange (e.g., a sweatshirt) to low-end (e.g., a bottle of Coke).

The team found that, on average, willingness to pay tripled when participants were feeling nostalgic. This effect was consistent across the various types of items that they looked at.

But why does this occur? The psychologists argued that there are two broad ways for people to get what they want in life: either through other people — what they call *social connectedness* — or money. Crucially, a focus on one of these routes crowds out the influence of the other. Since nostalgia boosts a sense of social connectedness, the importance of money wanes.

The experiment found that nostalgia generates such a large boost in willingness to pay that it's worth helping customers recall happy times from the past. Which is exactly what a Pumpkin Spice Latte does. Pumpkin pie is a beloved Thanksgiving dish and no family feast is complete without a slice for dessert. The distinctive spiced pumpkin flavor immediately transports us back in time, conjuring memories of childhood, home and family, evoking feelings of comfort and warmth. In other words: nostalgia.

So, it should come as no surprise that we're happy to purchase Starbucks' annual sweet treat.

What works in the world of coffee can work for you. Think about adding an element of nostalgia to your next campaign.

There are lots of different ways to do this. Perhaps you could set your ads in a bygone era to remind your audience of their childhood?

Or maybe you could harness familiar characters from yesteryear in your communications. This was the approach taken by Oreos when they partnered with Pac-Man for a limited edition. In multiple European markets they emblazoned packs, and the cookies inside, with characters and iconic elements from the game (like the maze). A simple promotional tactic to remind people of their youth and encourage them to spend more freely.

However you choose to use nostalgia, it's a powerful and simple tactic that can boost profitability.

THREE KEY TAKEAWAYS

1. **Add a limit to build demand**: Scarcity is consistently found to be one of the most important drivers of behavior. You can harness this bias by limiting the availability of your product in terms of either volume or time.

2. **Keep it special by taking it away**: Over time, the excitement with which people respond to your product will fade. Psychologists call this process *habituation*. Starbucks cleverly circumvents this challenge by removing PSL from sale before habituation occurs. Consider whether you can do the same for your product.

3. **Nostalgia opens folks' wallets**: Reminding people of their past in your communications can create a sense of nostalgia. That's beneficial, as nostalgic consumers tend to be less price sensitive.

3

SNICKERS

HUNGRY? FANCY SOME chocolate? Perhaps a Snickers bar would hit the spot?

A layer of chewy nougat, topped with peanuts and caramel and covered in milk chocolate, Snickers is the most loved chocolate bar in America. And there are some solid behavioral science findings that help to explain its success. So settle down with a sweet treat and read on to learn how the brand cornered the candy market.

A satisfying bite

Frank and Ethel Mars founded their chocolate company, Mars, in 1911, and had their first success with the Milky Way bar.

Still going strong in 1930, they launched Snickers. At the time, Mr and Mrs Mars were keen on horse racing — so much so that they'd bought up a large estate, which they named Milky Way Farm, so they could build their own race course. And when coming up with the name for their new candy creation, they decided to commemorate Ethel's favorite racehorse, Snickers, who had recently passed away.*

The main difference between Snickers and Milky Way bars was of course the peanuts. And it has always been sold as a satisfying bar, with its mix of nutty crunch and chewy nougat.

Frank Mars died in 1934, and Ethel five years later. But the company, and their chocolate bars, lived on. Since then, the confection has grown in popularity, and by 2013, the brand had passed $1 billion in annual sales.[10] And in 2025, Snickers is America's number one chocolate bar.[11]

"You're not you" – a marketing comeback

Central to Snickers' marketing has always been the idea of a snack that's more satisfying than the average candy.

This has generally worked well. About 15 years ago, however, the marketing lost its way. The brand's 2007 Super Bowl campaign about being 'manly' was accused of promoting stereotypes by the Gay and Lesbian Alliance Against Defamation (GLAAD). There were other attempts at promoting the masculine side of the bar. Unfortunately, this approach just didn't work, and is in part blamed for a 10% loss in market share between 2006 and 2009.[12]

By 2010, it was time for a reset. The first task for the team at BBDO — the agency appointed to the refresh — was to get to the heart of what makes Snickers so special. They conducted their own research, and this underlined the fact that Snickers, more than any other candy, really does fight hunger. Coupling this with the idea that our personalities genuinely change when we're hungry — we become sluggish, irritable, and unable to focus — the team came up with a new tagline, "You're not you when you're hungry."

---

* In the UK, the bar was known as a "Marathon" until 1990. Because Snickers sounds a bit too much like knickers — British slang for women's underwear.

CHAPTER 3: SNICKERS

The new campaign launched during the 2010 Super Bowl and featured beloved *Golden Girls* actress Betty White, then 89, and Abe Vigoda — who played Salvatore Tessio in *The Godfather* and was 88 at the time. The aging stars assume the roles of football players who are just too hungry to keep up with the game. But after a bite of Snickers, Betty transforms back to an athlete and is able to get on with the game. The premise being that when you're hungry, you're just not your normal self. The ad closes with the strapline, "You're not you when you're hungry. Snickers Satisfies."

The ads were an immediate hit — the brand had struck marketing gold. In its first full year, the campaign helped to increase global sales of Snickers by 15.9% and grew market share in 56 of the 58 markets in which it ran[13] — not bad for an 80-year-old, billion-dollar brand.

The "You're not you" campaign has won almost every industry accolade, including awards at Cannes, the Effies and the One Show.

Why has the campaign been so successful? Behavioral science can offer some clues.

A recognizable trigger

There's a well-known phenomenon in the field of psychology called the *intention-to-action gap*. That is, we often fail to take action despite our intention to do so. A prime example is the common experience of wanting to exercise, but not actually completing a workout. It suggests that motivation alone is often not enough to provoke a behavior.

One way to bridge the intention-to-action gap is to associate a behavior with a clear time, place or mood.

Some evidence for this comes from a 1997 study by Peter Gollwitzer and Veronika Brandstätter. The researchers asked participants to complete a simple task (to write a short report about their plans for Christmas Eve). Half of the group were asked to specify when and where they would complete the task. The other half were not asked to specify these details (the control group).

The results were stark: 32% of the control group completed the task, while a massive 71% of those who specified when and where they would write their report did so. Attaching the task to a clear time and place created a trigger moment which acted as a catalyst to convert vague intention into concrete action.

Other studies have found the same. In 2002, Sarah Milne, a psychologist at the University of Bath, assigned 248 participants to three groups. The control group were simply asked to record their exercise for two weeks. In this scenario, 35% exercised for 20 minutes at least once a week.

The second group were asked to record their exercise too, but they were also given a leaflet about the benefits of exercise, aimed at motivating them. The information boosted their intention to exercise — but barely shifted their behavior. Just 38% of this group exercised at least once a week, a tiny increase.

The third group recorded their exercise and received a motivational leaflet — and additionally had to state exactly when and where they would exercise. The motivation levels of this group were no different to the second group, but their behavior was: an impressive 91% of them exercised at least once a week. Milne argues that stating the time and place provided the participants with a self-defined trigger to remind them to exercise.

These studies show the power of creating a cue. If we say, "I'll do this on Tuesday morning after breakfast," for example, then when the Tuesday breakfast trigger rolls around, the task comes to mind, and we are far more likely to do it.

Why is this relevant to Snickers?

The "You're not you" campaign effectively builds a trigger moment — hunger — and connects it to a solution — Snickers. The ads remind us that any time we feel "hangry", that's the moment to reach for a Snickers bar. They encourage us to use hunger as a catalyst to convert a vague notion into action.

There are other, less subjective ways to create trigger moments. An example is one used by KitKat chocolate bars in the UK — "Have a break, have a KitKat," i.e., when it's time for your mid-morning coffee break, it's time for a KitKat. Diet Coke did something similar in the 1990s with their "Diet Coke Break" campaign, featuring muscled workmen taking shirtless morning breaks at 11:30 a.m. every working day.

Some of the most effective trigger-based campaigns describe a moment that arrives for everyone at the same time, or even a specific day of the week. A great example is Taco Tuesdays, which have been a US custom since the 1930s and offer a ready-made opportunity for brands like Taco Bell.

It's not just food brands that can apply this insight. Nationwide, a British bank,[*] ran a successful savings campaign with the strapline "PayDay = SaveDay."

Or for a larger-scale historical example, think back to the early days of Pepsodent. At the beginning of the 20th century, people were not yet in the habit of regular toothbrushing. Claude Hopkins, the creative brain behind Pepsodent's campaign, set out to change this. He aimed to persuade people to use their "dentifrice" more often — but he didn't simply suggest twice-daily toothbrushing. His ads recommended cleaning your teeth at two defined moments: after breakfast and before going to bed. By attaching the behavior to already-existing everyday routines, he framed these as triggers. And this could be hailed as one of the most successful campaigns ever, because the new habits he created are still followed 100 years later.

This emphasis on triggers, then, can be highly successful and save your campaigns from falling victim to the intention-to-action

---

[*] Technically Nationwide is a building society rather than a bank as it is owned by its members.

gap. Too many brands do the hard work of making their product appealing to boost motivation, but then fail to convert this to action with a trigger moment. So, think about what time, place or mood you can associate with your product.

A hint of humor

But the application of cues isn't Snickers' only successful use of behavioral science. It's the way they apply it as well — with humor.* The sight of various celebrities failing in everyday scenarios, like cutting wood or playing football, definitely evokes a chuckle.

Why does humor work?

Well, consider the word "advert." It's Latin for "turn towards," and captures a marketing fundamental. Gaining attention by cutting through the noise is the first job of any successful ad: as Leo Burnett, founder of one of the world's biggest ad agencies, said, "If you don't get noticed, you don't have anything."

Humor is a proven way to grab attention. Some evidence for this comes from a 2009 meta-analysis by Martin Eisend, professor of marketing at the European University Viadrina in Frankfurt. He reviewed 38 high-quality papers on the benefits of humor in ads, published between 1960 and 2004.

Eisend uncovered several statistically significant findings. And guess what was top of the list? Attention, which had the strongest positive correlation among a host of other benefits. Here's the list of factors most impacted by humor:

1. Attention
2. Attitude towards the ad

---

* Behavioral scientists do too. Why was Pavlov's hair so soft? Classical conditioning.

3. Lower negative emotion
4. Higher positive emotion
5. Purchase intent
6. Attitude towards the brand

The "You're not you" ads certainly grabbed and held the viewer's attention. And as you can see, there are plenty of other reasons to consider a more light-hearted tone for your brand.

There's one other — less widely discussed — advantage to using humor: reducing price sensitivity. Being in a good mood seems to increase what people are willing to pay. In 2023, Richard carried out his own study, with Ben Saxon at News UK and Chris Davies at Carat, to test the scale of this impact.

They showed 821 respondents two different ads (one for a pizza and beer deal, one for a bottle of Baileys). Participants were asked how they would rate the value of the offer on a scale from one to five (one = very poor value; five = very good value). They were also asked to rate their mood.

> When people are feeling upbeat, they focus on the benefits a brand will bring.

Results showed that when people were in a bad or very bad mood, 60% thought the product was good or great value. However, among those claiming to be in a good or very good mood that figure jumped to 76% — a 26% improvement. It seems that when people are feeling upbeat, they focus on the benefits a brand will bring. But when they're feeling grumpy, they pay more attention to the opportunity costs of spending money.

Telling advertisers about the importance of humor might sound like stating the obvious. But it's a simple lesson that has been forgotten by the industry. Figures from the market research company Kantar show that the proportion of ads across the globe that use humor dropped from 53% in 2000 to 34% in 2024. Advertisers are ignoring the evidence for levity and becoming far too solemn.

But what's bad for the industry is good for you. If you add a dash of wit to your ads, not only will you benefit in the ways outlined here, you'll also be distinctive. And, as we discuss in the Liquid Death chapter, that's one of the surest ways of grabbing attention.

Comedy fine print

The example of Snickers doesn't just show *why* you should use humor, it also demonstrates *how*.

One of the most successful aspects of "You're not you" is that the candy is so integral to the joke. That's crucial. Otherwise you're in danger of the *vampire effect*. This is the finding that jokes unrelated to the brand can backfire. In these instances, the viewer's attention is sucked away from the commercial message towards the punchline.

To paraphrase the creative director Bill Bernbach:

> You are NOT right if in your ad you stand a man on his head JUST to get [a laugh]. You ARE right if you have him on his head to show how your product keeps things from falling out of his pockets.

That argument is supported by Kantar's LINK data. Their research, illustrated in Chart 2, shows that there is a dramatic difference in both the short-term and long-term effectiveness of funny ads — depending on how connected the joke is to the brand.

Chart 2: The most effective ads connect their humor to the brand

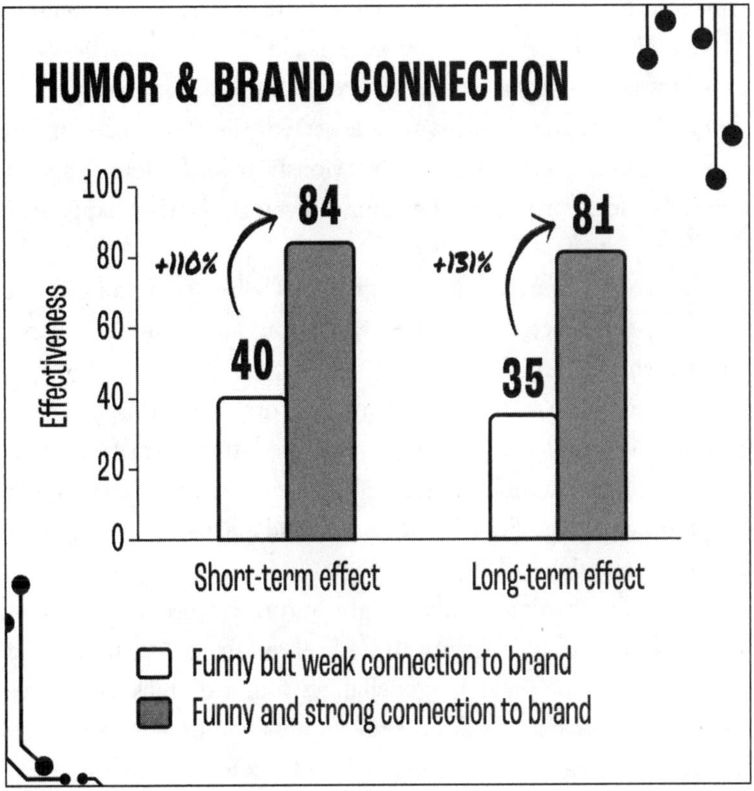

HUMOR & BRAND CONNECTION

Effectiveness

Short-term effect: 40 (Funny but weak connection to brand) → 84 (Funny and strong connection to brand), +110%

Long-term effect: 35 → 81, +131%

☐ Funny but weak connection to brand
■ Funny and strong connection to brand

Source: Adapted from Kantar LINK Database (2024).

Snickers create this connection brilliantly. The ads wouldn't work if you removed the product. Snickers is central to the joke — it's only when the bar is consumed that the character returns to normal. So, when you're considering how to generate a laugh with your ads, make sure you keep it relevant.

You might want to consider the type of joke featured in the Snickers ads too. It's called *incongruity*, and has been a well-understood facet of humor since a study dating back to 1970.

Göran Nerhardt at the University of Stockholm conducted an

experiment into the effect of incongruent expectations on laughter. He recruited participants and handed them a series of weights. After they held each one, they were asked to judge how heavy or light it was on a six-point scale from very light to very heavy.

Finally, they were handed an unexpectedly light weight — much lighter than the ones they had previously held. It doesn't sound remotely funny when described, but can you guess what happened? People chuckled.

Nerhardt reasoned that incongruity — when something is out of place, unexpected or defies what you anticipate — sparks amusement.

Snickers' "You're not you" campaign draws on this principle. The ads illustrate exaggerated, unexpected transformations that disrupt our expectations of normal behavior. Seeing Betty White on a football field defies what we expect and creates an incongruous scenario that triggers laughter.

Just as Nerhardt's lighter weight surprise caused amusement, Snickers' ads use incongruity to both entertain and reinforce the brand's central message: hunger changes you, and Snickers restores you to your normal self. And if the ad puts you in a good enough mood, maybe you'll hop off the couch and pop to the store for a treat.

Clearly, humor is not just a laughing matter. As actor Peter Ustinov once said, "Comedy is simply a funny way of being serious."

CHAPTER 3: SNICKERS

THREE KEY TAKEAWAYS

1. **Pair desire with a trigger**: Motivation alone is not enough. If you only create desire for your product you might fall victim to the intention-to-action gap. Instead, make sure you complement product appeal with a clear cue or trigger for consumption. Snickers does this by associating their product with the personality changes that come from hunger. Can you think of a time, place, or mood you could associate with your brand?

2. **Use humor to persuade**: There are solid psychological and business reasons for communicating in a light-hearted way. It grabs attention and persuades people to part with their money. The fact that marketers have turned away from laughter is an opportunity for you. It's rare to find a tactic that is both well proven and rarely used.

3. **Keep jokes on-brand**: Make sure you're funny in a way that is relevant to your brand. Humor backfires when it's shoehorned into the ad. In this setting, the joke can overshadow the brand message, a problem known as the vampire effect.

4

APPLE

Take a look at your desk. Or your hand. Is there an Apple device sitting there? If so, you're one of over two billion users worldwide.[14] And there's barely a person on the planet who hasn't heard of Apple. How's that for brand penetration?

There are, of course, many reasons for Apple's epic success. Let's take a look at a couple here, which reflect some interesting behavioral insights.

An Apple seed that bears fruit

Apple launched its first personal computer — the Apple-1 — in 1976. Built by hand by Steve Wozniak, it cost $666.66 — which seems reasonable, except that in today's money that's almost $3,700. Strictly for computer nerds, it allowed you to write simple code and play a basic game or two. In fact, you needed to be a nerd just to understand the ads, crammed as they were with all the details about its 24-line video display, on-board RAM capacity of 8K BYTES and new 16-pin 4K RAM chips. Few had a clue what all this meant.

Wozniak claims he built the Apple-1 simply to prove he could. You could argue that this underlying sense of superiority remained part of the brand when he and Steve Jobs teamed up, ushering in a bold new vision for the future of computing.

Fast forward half a century and Apple has become an icon, touching the lives of billions of fans.

For the first 20 years or so, Apple focused on personal and home computing; but in 2001, it launched what would become one of its most well-loved inventions — the iPod. MP3 players were already becoming popular, as they allowed music fans to listen to a personalized mix of tracks rather than a pre-recorded collection. But they were clunky and low capacity.

The iPod changed this. It had a slick scroll-wheel that allowed you to flip quickly through all your tunes — and, more importantly, it offered huge storage. And by forcing users to download through iTunes, it reduced the music piracy that was rife at the time, thereby keeping artists and labels happy too.

But what drove its popularity? One factor was Apple's legendary advertising and, in particular, the way it exploited an important behavioral insight.

Can you picture your pocket?

To understand why the iPod ads were so effective, it helps to understand the context. Other MP3 players were available. One example was the Philips RUSH digital audio player, which launched in 2000. The headline for the print ads was "MP3 in full motion," followed by a bullet list of features, such as "Built-in memory capacity: 128 MB" and "Plays MP3 and WMA digital audio."

Contrast this with Apple's approach: a large image of the sleek, white design and the headline: "1,000 songs. In your pocket." The ad allows us to immediately grasp the storage concept, because it's far easier to understand songs than megabytes. And, of course, we understand that it's small and sleek. We can imagine carrying the device in our jeans as we go about our lives with a soundtrack in our ears. The ad is immediately impactful and memorable.

But why, exactly?

The creative makes use of a bias called *concreteness*. That is, we are far more likely to recall concrete things — things that we can see in our mind's eye — than abstract ideas. There's consistent evidence to support this.

Let's dig into the research. One of the original studies into concreteness was carried out by Ian Begg at the University of Western Ontario in 1972. He recruited 25 students and read them a list of 20 two-word phrases, such as:

square door
impossible amount
rusty engine
better excuse
flaming forest
apparent fact
muscular gentleman
common fate
white horse
subtle fault

Then he asked the group to remember as many terms as they could. You could even try the challenge yourself right now. If you struggle, don't worry. In the study, participants recalled an average of 23% of the terms.

But Begg made a striking observation. People remembered just 9% of the abstract words, such as "impossible amount," versus 36% of the concrete terms, such as "white horse." That's a fourfold difference.

Why? Begg argued that vision is the most powerful of our senses, so when you can picture something in your head, such as a white horse, you find it much easier to hang on to that thought.

If you're wondering whether the results hold in a more commercial setting, and among a more representative audience, you're not alone. So in 2021, Richard, together with Mike Treharne, head of insight at Leo Burnett, conducted a further study to see if they could replicate the findings.

They recruited a larger sample of 425 people and gave them a list of ten phrases, some abstract and some concrete. They were all word pairs that could feasibly appear in commercial communications, such as those in Table 3.

Table 3: The phrases used in the concreteness study

CONCRETE	ABSTRACT
fast car	innovative quality
skinny jeans	trusted provenance
cashew nut	central purpose
money in your pocket	wholesome nutrition
happy hens	ethical vision

Source: Shotton and Treharne (2021).

When asked to recall as many words as possible five minutes later, the results were even starker than in the original study. Subjects remembered just 0.7% of the abstract phrases, and 6.7% of the concrete ones — a near tenfold difference. So, it's clear that Begg's findings about concreteness still hold and are likely to be effective in ads.

Avoiding the abstract and choosing words we can visualize works because sight is a powerful and complex sense. We can take the additional processing step of conjuring an image in our minds in a way that we can't do with a word like "innovation." And this additional processing is enough to allow us to hold the word in our memories for longer.

Apple showed us a pocket-sized product and invited us to imagine the iPod nestled in our jeans. In doing so, it made it memorable. Apple also turned an incomprehensible 5GB into 1,000 songs — a far more concrete image.

This technique is ignored too often by marketers. Think about the brand claims that you encounter most often: "premium," "trustworthy," "high quality," and the like. These attributes are fine as internal objectives, but they fail when used in public communications. Your customer can understand them but will forget them almost immediately.

Avoid ambiguous abstract terms — instead, think of a *thing* that your customers can conjure in their mind's eye. And use that word. There are plenty of examples beyond Apple. Consider Red Bull. They could have used "Red Bull Gives you Energy" — but there's nothing for your imagination to latch onto in that. "Red Bull Gives you Wings" on the other hand, and you can picture yourself flying. Other brands that have done this well include "Skittles — Taste The Rainbow," "M&Ms — Melt in Your Mouth, Not in Your Hand," and "Maxwell House — Good to the Last Drop."

The principle of concreteness can be applied beyond copywriting. There's a lateral approach that you could consider: the use of a *fluent device*. This is a term coined by Orlando Wood at research agency System1 to describe "[a] fictitious character or characters (humans or creatures) created by the brand and used as the primary vehicle for the drama in more than one ad across a campaign."

Fluent devices include characters like Tony the Tiger, the Aflac duck, and the Jolly Green Giant. They've been at the heart of some of the most effective American ad campaigns ever. The same is true in the UK: consider the success of the 118 118 runners, Aleksandr the Meerkat, or the Smash Martians.

These devices work because they harness concreteness. If you're GEICO, it's very hard to get people to remember that you offer value for money; it's too abstract a concept. But the GEICO Gecko — a talking lizard that embodies those ideas? Unforgettable.

Of course, it's easy to pick a handful of case studies to support a theory. But the evidence for fluent devices goes beyond that. System1 analyzed 335 campaigns from the biannual Institute of Practitioners in Advertising Effectiveness Awards database (the UK's leading ad award body) to test their impact.

> Campaigns with a fluent device are 32% more likely to achieve large market share gain.

You can see the results in Chart 3: campaigns with a fluent device are 32% more likely to achieve large market share gain than those without.

Of course, we all know that correlation does not equal causation — it could just be that those campaigns are better executed. But the theory of concreteness would suggest that these techniques do at least play a part. Fluent devices are highly visual, concrete and thus memorable.

Chart 3: Using a fluent device increased campaign effectiveness

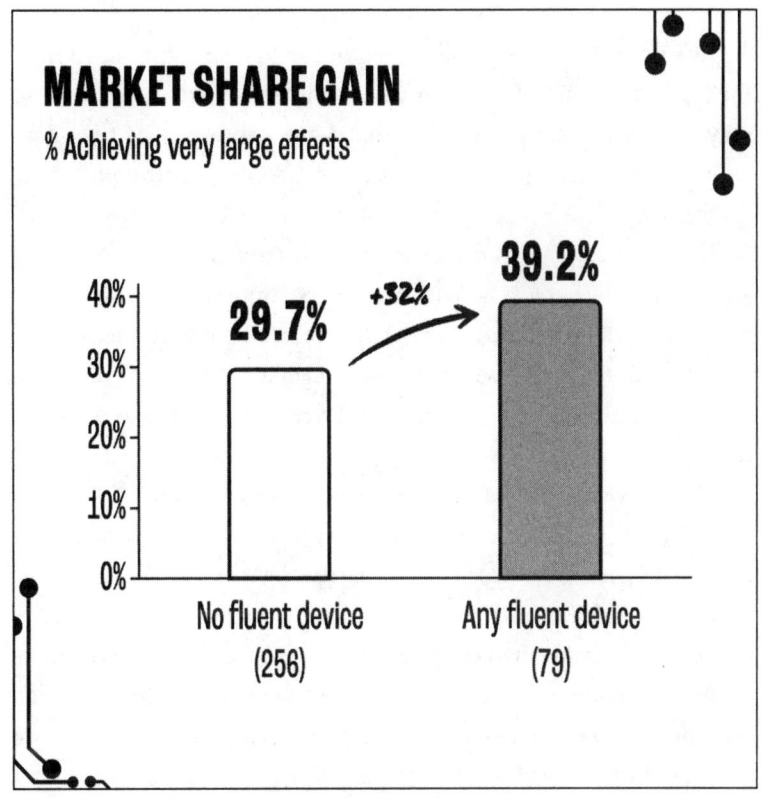

Source: Adapted from System1 (2019).

Despite the effectiveness of fluent devices, few advertisers are taking advantage of them. According to System1, only 4% of ads in the US and 7% in Britain now use them — a far cry from their heyday in the early 1990s, when almost half of ads (41%) in the UK used fluent devices.

What's bad for the general effectiveness of advertising is good for you. After all, it means that if you introduce a fluent device to your advertising, you'll be distinctive — and we know that distinctiveness is key to noticeability.

Navigating novelty

Apple's iPod success paved the way for the first smartphone. Before then, we used our phones to make calls, send text messages, and maybe play the snake game. Perhaps send an email or two. And we were comfortable with the idea of pressing buttons to make things happen.

Then, in 2007, the iPhone arrived. With a touchscreen. And barely any buttons. What?! It was not an understatement when Steve Jobs said that with this new device, "Apple reinvents the phone."

How did Apple persuade us to take that leap into the technological unknown? The challenge was to make it seem more "known."

Do we want familiar things? Yes, we do. There's evidence to show that the most successful innovations are those that strike a balance between novelty and familiarity.

For example, in 2013, Brian Uzzi from Northwestern University carried out a meta-analysis of 17.9 million scientific research papers to examine how well received studies with novel content were. To do this, he examined two different categories of studies: those that combined novel ideas with familiar concepts and those that primarily focused on new insights. Uzzi calculated the number of times papers in each group were cited by other authors.

There was a clear winner: papers that balanced novelty and familiarity were twice as likely to be referenced in later work than papers that emphasized novel ideas. This suggests that, even at the cutting edge of science, people prefer somewhat familiar concepts to radically new thinking.

Another piece of research from 2012 found a similar phenomenon. Kevin Boudreau of London Business School led a team that looked at which types of research proposals, ranging from novel to familiar, were most likely to win funding.

To this end, the researchers asked 142 world-class scientists from a US medical school to evaluate 15 funding proposals on a ten-point scale (one = least impact; ten = most impact).

The results revealed that the scientists assigned the lowest scores to the most novel ideas. Proposals about research that was already highly familiar scored only slightly higher. However, when proposals were slightly new, yet not entirely novel, they received the highest evaluation. Boudreau describes this as *optimal newness*.

Keep us comfortable with change

The best innovators have long understood the idea of treading a careful line between the old and the new. Take the example of the lightbulb. When Thomas Edison came up with his invention, he had an instinctive understanding not only of the power of electricity, but also of the need to bring people along with him. He realized that disruptive ideas can excite and terrify in equal measure — and that fear might slow the uptake of the new technology.

According to a 2001 paper by Andrew Hargadon of the University of California, Davis, Edison intentionally put people's minds at ease by keeping his electric bulb closely aligned with the gas lighting of the day.

In his notebooks, Edison wrote that he intended to "effect exact imitation of all done by gas, so as to replace lighting by gas with lighting by electricity … not to make a large light or a blinding light, but a small light having the mildness of gas."

So, he created bulbs with roughly the same brightness as a gas lamp, and finished them off with a light shade — used to stop gas lamps flickering in a draft, but arguably unnecessary for electricity. He even insisted on putting electric cables underground — the same as gas pipes.

Most advanced yet acceptable

Edison's conscious decision to align electric bulbs with gas lighting is an early example of the principle of MAYA: most advanced yet acceptable. This was first described by the industrial designer Raymond Loewy, who is credited with some of the world's most recognizable designs, including the Shell logo, the Lucky Strike packaging, and Air Force One's livery.

According to Loewy, it is important to design for the future — but gradually, and in keeping with the present: "The adult public's taste is not necessarily ready to accept the logical solutions to their requirements if the solution implies too vast a departure from what they have been conditioned into accepting as the norm."

There is experimental evidence to suggest that this approach was right. In 2003, Paul Hekkert led a study at the Delft University of Technology to test the MAYA principle.

He asked participants to look at items in one of three different product categories: sanders (where aesthetic design isn't important), telephones, and kettles (where design matters more). Items in each category represented varying levels of typicality and novelty: some items were typical in their appearance, some were novel and others fell somewhere in between.

Participants were asked to rate these items in terms of how usual or original they were, as well as how much they liked the item. This allowed Hekkert to examine the influence of typicality and novelty on appeal.

The results showed that people placed equal importance on novelty as they did on typicality, preferring products that had an optimal combination of both aspects — which confirms the MAYA principle.

This is characteristic of the designs seen when iPhones first launched. The device was unlike any phone seen before, so Apple kept as many elements as reassuringly recognizable as possible.

The Notes icon resembled a page of yellow-lined note paper; the Newsstand was a wooden shelf; the Game Center removed any doubt about its function by featuring a chessboard and baseball icons; and everything had a 3D look to it, helping us get over the fact that these were not actual buttons.

This is a design technique called *skeuomorphism*, whereby digital elements are made to look like real-world objects.

The skeuomorphic design helped us understand and accept the array of new icons and functions that would soon come to punctuate almost every aspect of our daily lives, from morning alarm to bedtime reading and everything in between.

But skeuomorphism isn't right for every brief, remember it's *optimal* newness that Boudreau recommends. If your product is already familiar then skeuomorphism is probably inappropriate.

Again, the example of Apple is instructive. By the time iOS 7 was launched in 2013, the technology was no longer radical, so they toned down the use of skeuomorphs and applied a more minimalist approach.

The task for you as a marketer is to honestly reflect on how ground-breaking your product is. If you can answer that accurately then the right design tactic becomes clear.

In the words of *Atlantic* columnist Derek Thompson: "[T]o sell something surprising, make it familiar; and to sell something familiar, make it surprising." This is what Apple did.

THREE KEY TAKEAWAYS

1. **What you can see will be remembered**: Apply the principle of concreteness to make your words more memorable. Always try to include visualizable objects instead of — or in support of — abstract words and concepts.

2. **Mascots matter**: Consider using a fluent device – a character that's central across a campaign can be a powerful way to enhance memorability and effectiveness.

3. **Balance newness with familiarity**: Keep in mind the principle of optimal newness, and aim to strike a balance between novelty and familiarity when introducing new products, services, or ideas.

5

AMAZON PRIME

What have you ordered from Amazon this week? A book? Cat food? Compression socks? Or, maybe, all of the above?

How did Amazon become such a commercial behemoth? Behavioral science played a part.

It seems to be an area that founder Jeff Bezos has always been interested in, with his instinctive awareness of the need to address the unchanging facets of humanity. He once said:

> I very frequently get the question: "What's going to change in the next ten years?" And that is a very interesting question; it's a very common one. I almost never get the question: "What's not going to change in the next ten years?" And I submit to you that that second question is actually the more important of the two — because you can build a business strategy around the things that are stable in time.

Let's take a look at how Amazon has crafted some of its most enduring, long-term strategies around human behavior.

From garage to global

Jeff Bezos started Amazon from his garage in July 1995. In fact, it wasn't Amazon then; it was Cadabra. But his attorney misheard this as "cadaver," so Bezos had a rethink. He landed on "Amazon" because it suggested scale and because back then, website listings were alphabetical. He wanted to lead, right from the beginning.

Always interested in technology, Bezos started his career at fintech startup Fitel. At 30, he decided to strike out with his own venture. Starting small, he built a company grounded in technological innovation.

Amazon was originally established as an online bookseller, but Bezos always had big dreams. His aim was to go global and supply everything to everyone, everywhere.

And in this, he's succeeded. Amazon is an unstoppable juggernaut: the world's largest online retailer at the time of writing (with approximately 83% of US households shopping there and spending nearly $638 billion every year), where you can get almost anything you can imagine — often less than 24 hours after you think of it.[15]

What biases have helped Bezos become one of the world's richest people?

Prime time

One of the most important drivers of this astronomical growth has been Amazon Prime. This was the first-ever such membership program: for a one-off, upfront fee, customers could get two-day delivery as often as they wished over a year.

Prime launched in 2005, although it had initially faced resistance from top management, who feared over-keen customers could bankrupt the company.

There are now almost 200 million Prime subscribers around the world.[16] This includes two out of three internet users in America;[17] and with each one paying around $139 a year, that's an enormous revenue stream.

But perhaps even more importantly, Prime members spend more than non-Prime customers — the average Prime member spends $110 on Amazon every month, versus just $38 for non-members.[18]

Some people argue that this is just a factor of heavier spenders being more likely to pay for the service. And that could be part of it. But there is also a psychological bias that means people tend to spend more if they have made an upfront payment: the *sunk cost fallacy*. This is defined as a tendency to continue investing simply because money, effort, or time has already been expended. Essentially, the prior investment motivates the decision to keep on spending — even though, objectively, it should not.

It's called a "fallacy" because it's not necessarily rational. So, why do we "throw good money after bad?"

"I've already paid for delivery"

There's a wealth of evidence to show this phenomenon is real. One of the original experiments was carried out in 1985 by Hal Arkes and Catherine Blumer at Ohio University. They asked participants to imagine the following scenario:

> Assume that you have spent $100 on a ticket for a weekend ski trip to Michigan. Several weeks later, you buy a $50 ticket for a ski trip to Wisconsin. You think you will enjoy the Wisconsin ski trip more than the Michigan ski trip. As you are putting your just-purchased Wisconsin ski trip ticket in your wallet, you notice that the Michigan ski trip and the Wisconsin ski trip are for the same weekend! It's too late to

sell either ticket, and you cannot return either one. You must use one ticket and not the other.

Participants were then asked: "Which trip will you go on?" Essentially, they had to choose between two clashing holidays, a fantastic cheap one or an adequate, but expensive, one. Since the tickets had already been bought and the money wasn't recoverable, the answer should have been obvious. Pick the fantastic one. Go to Wisconsin.

But that's not what happened: only a minority went for Wisconsin (at 46%). The majority (54%) opted for the pricier Michigan trip.

Picking the more expensive, but less enjoyable, weekend is an example of the sunk cost fallacy — people tend to pursue options with the greatest past investment.

You might be questioning whether we should generalize from a thought experiment. Arkes and Blumer did too, so they followed up with a real-world study among theatergoers.

They targeted people lining up to buy season tickets for the Ohio University Theater. The tickets were being advertised as costing $15, but when the prospective buyers reached the front of the line they were offered one of three random prices:

1. The standard $15;
2. A slightly discounted $13; or
3. A heavily discounted $8.

The researchers then monitored how many shows the season ticket holders attended over the next six months. The findings are shown in Table 4.

Table 4: The higher the ticket price, the stronger the sunk cost fallacy

AMOUNT PAID FOR SEASON TICKET	NUMBER OF PERFORMANCES ATTENDED (AVERAGE)
$15	4.11
$13	3.32
$8	3.29

+25% (between $8 and $15)

Source: Adapted from Arkes and Blumer (1985).

The results revealed that those who had spent the most on their tickets attended the most plays (4.11 on average). To be precise, this group went to 25% more shows than those who only paid $8. The researchers reasoned that people who had paid the full price attended more plays because they had the highest sunk costs. They were most motivated to get their money's worth.

Theater season tickets aren't exactly a mainstream product, so we wanted to test the principle in a more typical commercial setting. Along with Jon Puleston, Nicki Morley, and Max Wiggins at the research agency Kantar, we recruited more than 500 British participants to take part in an experiment.

We asked half the participants to imagine they were about to buy a book they had been interested in for a while. They could either pay £8.99 on Amazon and receive the book today or pay £6.99 with WHSmith (a well-known British retailer) but receive it tomorrow. In that setting, only 37% of people paid the premium and went with Amazon. The majority would rather pay £2 less and wait a day.

The second half of respondents were given the same basic choice: £8.99 for same-day delivery from Amazon or £6.99 for next-day from WHSmith. But additionally, this group was told to imagine that they had bought an Amazon Prime subscription for £95 earlier in the year.

In that setting, even though the underlying question was the same — "Do you want to pay a premium to get the book quicker?" — the number who were prepared to spend more went up to 40% — an 8% increase. The thought of "wasting" the subscription fee inclined them to opt for Amazon.

Multiple studies support this finding. In a 2015 meta-analysis of 98 studies conducted by Stefan Roth at the University of Kaiserslautern in Germany, the sunk cost effect was identified across a diverse range of businesses, from gambling to all-you-can-eat buffets. The bias was particularly strong among younger people, which is something to consider if that's your key audience.

A change in behavior

What's going on? An obvious explanation is that we hate to feel we're "wasting" money. We've spent some cash and we want to get our money's worth.

Hal Arkes, co-author of the ski-trip study discussed in the previous section, goes further with his explanation. He suggests that the sunk cost fallacy arises because if we were to stop investing after an initial outlay, this would constitute an admission that our expenditure was foolish. We can't accept this, so we continue to act as if the original spend was sensible, emphasizing this by splashing out more on the same thing.

This explains why Prime works so well. Once purchased, customers will go to illogical lengths to feel they're getting their money's worth. The question you need to ask is how can you emulate Amazon?

One option would be a subscription program that covers deliveries upfront, like Amazon. That's what Uber Eats does with its Uber One program. You pay a $9.99 fee to cover all deliveries across the month.

If delivery doesn't work for your business, you could take the approach of Sweetgreen — an American salad restaurant, which offers a pass for $10 a month that will earn you $3 credit for every visit. The math for the customer is simple: all you have to do is visit more than three times a month. But it pays off for the company, too. According to Sweetgreen's chief digital officer, Daniel Schlossman, it's been a hit: "We saw that, no matter what type of customer you were, you came back more often in that [subscription] period." And you can bet that for each visit, customers will be spending more than the $3 they get in return.

Another example is Club Pret from sandwich chain Pret A Manger, in the UK. For a monthly fee you get five coffees a day at half price. This harnesses the sunk cost effect. Let's say Pret normally charges £4 a coffee and members pay just £2 a time. If an equally good coffee shop opened up next door charging £1.75, the sunk cost fallacy suggests people will continue buying at Pret.

Timely reminders

When Amazon first introduced its subscription, annual payment was the only option. Now there's a monthly option. There is evidence that, whatever format you decide on for your subscription model, simply having customers make a regular payment will increase consumption. One study examining this was conducted in 1998 by John Gourville of Harvard University and Dilip Soman at the University of Colorado.

The researchers analyzed data on the payment and attendance of 200 gym goers in Colorado. They could pay annually, semi-annually, quarterly, or monthly.

The results showed that members who made annual payments

visited the gym the most in the months following payment, with visits then gradually dropping off. A similar pattern was seen for semi-annual and quarterly members.

However, for monthly members, gym use was more consistent. These people were reminded of the cost of their membership every month, so they felt the need to get their money's worth.

So, an additional aspect of subscriptions is that they can do a good job of keeping a brand or product front of mind.

And there's another bias related to sunk costs that might help you out when planning your subscription program: the *illusion of progress*. Because it's not just monetary investment that we're unwilling to give up on — but effort too. This is nicely captured by the phrase, "I've started so I'll finish." Even where outcomes may become worse if we continue an action, we are motivated not to give up simply due to the time we've already put in.

Evidence that this tactic can work in a commercial setting comes from Ran Kivetz at Columbia Business School. In 2006, he distributed loyalty cards to drinkers at a cafe. Some received a card with ten empty stamp spaces which, once full, would earn the participants a free cup of coffee. Others were given a 12-stamp version with two stamps already filled in.

Even though both sets of drinkers needed to buy ten cups to get a freebie, they behaved differently. Those with the empty ten-stamp version completed their cards in 15.6 days, while participants with the partially-filled 12-stamp version finished their cards in 12.7 days — a difference of 19%. Notably, participants also accelerated their coffee consumption when they got closer to receiving their free cup.

The way to harness this is to remind your customers of any effort they've already put in while engaging with your brand. Let's say you have a loyalty program in which you offer people a $5 reward once they have 500 points. Based on Kivetz's study, you should change that process so that you give people a $5 reward after they have reached 600 points — but give them the first 100 points free at the start.

Or imagine an e-commerce site selling shoes. Once shoppers have added an item to the basket, a bar appears indicating they have two more steps to complete: adding address details and making payment. The implication of Kivetz's study is to change the visual so that it indicates that there are three steps, but one has already been completed (selecting the item), with two remaining (adding address details and making payment).

These are low-cost interventions that can have significant effects.

Price is a charm

The sunk cost fallacy is not the only bias that Amazon has built its business on. Many others have come into play — not least, *charm pricing*.

Of course, whole books could be written about Amazon's approach to pricing. But there's a neat trick that Amazon has employed right from the start for its subscription pricing: the amount always ends with a nine. This is called charm pricing and it works surprisingly well for such a simple detail.

Richard carried out his own research looking at whether charm pricing influences value perceptions. He surveyed 650 UK consumers, showing them items with prices that either ended in 99p (e.g., £5.99) or were rounded to the nearest pound (e.g., £6). Participants were asked whether the items seemed like good value. The results showed that items with charm prices were 9% more likely to be viewed as good value than those with rounded prices. This difference is disproportionate to the actual price drop.

Other larger studies have found the same. For example, in 2023, Avner Shlain from Berkeley led a study into the effect of charm pricing. He analyzed retail scanner data from thousands of products and found that people perceived prices ending in 99 as being a massive 15–25 cents lower than the rounded price, despite only being one cent lower in reality. So, $5.99 can "feel like" $5.75.

Amazon makes the most of this. When it first launched Prime, the annual cost was $79. When a monthly payment option was introduced in 2016, it was priced at $10.99. In 2022, the price was $14.99 a month or $139 a year. Every monthly fee for Amazon Prime has been a charm price.

Coupled with a subscription that feels like it offers free delivery, Amazon Prime customers are given a sense of good value when they shop there. And as Jeff Bezos said:

> It's impossible to imagine a future ten years from now where a customer comes up and says, 'Jeff, I love Amazon; I just wish the prices were a little higher,' … Impossible. And so the effort we put into those things, spinning those things up, we know the energy we put into it today will still be paying off dividends for our customers ten years from now.

The brand offers a prime example, if you will, of how the application of some apparently small behavioral science ideas can stack up to a big difference.

CHAPTER 5: AMAZON PRIME

THREE KEY TAKEAWAYS

1. **Use upfront costs to encourage engagement**: Prompt shoppers to make an initial investment — like paying for an ongoing discount. If they do, the sunk cost fallacy suggests they'll keep on buying your products even when there are objectively better alternatives.

2. **Remind people what they've started**: Highlight your customer's progress — even if it's artificially boosted. Doing so will increase the likelihood they keep on buying. It taps into our desire not to "waste" prior effort.

3. **Price smart with charm pricing**: Make sure to use charm pricing. If you have any products that are sold for a round amount, a one cent reduction will make them appear significantly better value.

6

APEROL

DID YOU SIP an Aperol Spritz this past summer?
If you're someone who enjoys the occasional cocktail, there's a strong chance you've at least tried one — even if you decided the bitterness wasn't for you and didn't order one again.

Why? Well, there are some powerful behavioral biases that may have influenced you.

A Mediterranean heritage

In 1912, two Italian brothers — Luigi and Silvio Barbieri — inherited their father's liquor business and wanted to create something new.

After what you could imagine was a rather fun seven years of research, they landed upon a new recipe, using a unique combination of citrus, spice, and herb essences. They called it Aperol, after the French colloquialism for aperitif: *apero*.

Aperol was launched to a receptive audience at the 1919 Padua International Fair, offering a slightly lower-alcohol alternative to other aperitifs on the market. In fact, its relatively low 11% ABV was one of the early selling points. The drink was aimed at "women and sportive people." Presumably, at the time, boozy evenings for sportspeople were the norm — but they had to draw the line somewhere.

The Aperol recipe remains a closely guarded secret. It's a complex mix with a bitter finish, and for some a touch too intense. Which is where the spritz comes in.

The Aperol Spritz — inspired by the German *spritzer* (splash) — was born in the 1950s, combining two parts Aperol, three parts Italian prosecco, plus a dash of soda water. It quickly became a popular drink for any *aperitivo* occasion across Italy.

But it wasn't until later that the popularity of the Aperol Spritz spread to the US and the UK.

Colorful growth

When Campari bought the Aperol brand in 2003, the company began to invest in advertising. It started with a big push in New York, with Aperol Spritz booths popping up at summertime events like the Governors Ball and the Jazz Age Lawn Party.

Campari wrapped a Hampton Jitney bus in bright orange branding, bringing Aperol to the attention of wealthy weekenders. Around the Hamptons, a little scooter became a mobile Aperol bar, zipping about serving free spritzes.

The orange vibes broke through, and the drink began to catch on across the US and then the UK. Around 2015, there was a slight peak in interest as measured by Google search volumes; and by 2017, those vibrant cocktails were on everyone's lips.

Chart 4: Searches for "Aperol Spritz" began to increase in late 2015

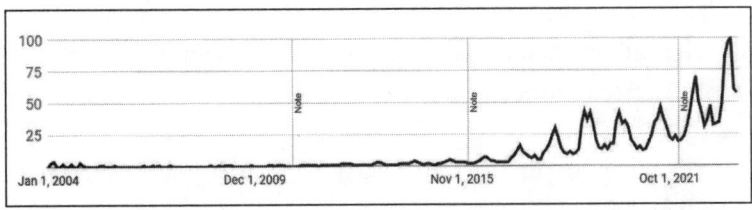

Source: Google Trends (2025).

So, what's going on?

There's something special about Aperol, apart from the taste: its distinctive, zesty orange color. There's really no other drink like it. When you see someone drinking Aperol, you know it couldn't be anything else — especially if it's poured into a generously proportioned Aperol balloon glass.

It's this visual distinctiveness that has driven Aperol's success, by tapping into one of the most influential of behavioral biases: *social proof*. This is the idea that when a behavior seems popular, it becomes more appealing, so people are more likely to adopt it.

It's a timesaving, pragmatic approach to decision-making. If a screaming horde runs out of a building, social proof dictates that we follow them. Sensible. When you find yourself at a crowded bar, the pressure to order quickly is intense, and often the choice isn't clear. In that setting, copying others is an easy decision-making shortcut.

As Robert Cialdini, professor of marketing and psychology at Arizona State University, says:

> When a behavior seems popular, it becomes more appealing, so people are more likely to adopt it.

If a lot of people are doing the same thing, they must know something we don't. Especially when we are uncertain, we are willing to place an enormous amount of trust in the collective knowledge of the crowd.

There's a lot of empirical evidence supporting the idea of social proof.

One study comes from the British tax office, His Majesty's Revenue & Customs (HMRC). In 2012, it sent out 140,000 letters testing different messages to see which ones improved tax repayment rates. When these letters simply told people about their legal obligation to pay their taxes and informed them of the risk of a fine, 68% complied. However, when the letters included a social proof message telling people that "nine out of ten people in [the local area] pay their tax on time," the payment rate jumped to 83%. Essentially, if everyone's doing something, we want to as well.

This tactic is regularly applied by advertisers. Think of all those messages you see about Oreos selling by the million or Bud Light being the nation's favorite beer. That's social proof in practice. If your marketing doesn't do this already, give it a go. The evidence suggests you'll boost sales.

But the twist with Aperol is that the brand doesn't directly state its popularity; instead, the drink's distinctive design naturally makes its consumption highly visible. Once people started to drink the cocktail, Aperol, the drink caught on quickly because it was so noticeable. If it had been a colorless liquid, observers wouldn't be able to tell what others were drinking — it could be vodka, gin, rum, or tequila.

It might feel like a stretch to imply that such a subtle use of social proof can work, but there's evidence this is a highly persuasive approach. In a 2008 study, University of Groningen researchers Kees Keizer and Siegwart Lindenberg, investigated the effect of *implied social proof* on littering in the Netherlands.

CHAPTER 6: APEROL

The team identified an alleyway where many bikes were parked and attached flyers for a fictitious sports shop to the handlebars. Crucially, there were no trash cans in the area. They then covertly monitored how the owners of the bikes dealt with the flyers.

There were two setups in the study. In the first, the researchers cleaned up the alleyway, clearing away garbage to make it nice and neat. In the second, they scattered bits of trash on the ground and added graffiti to the walls.

The results were stark. When the alley was clean — with the implied social norm that most people took their garbage home with them — only 33% of cyclists dropped the flyers on the ground. However, in the messy setup, suggesting that littering is commonplace, 69% of people discarded the flyers inappropriately.

This study, and others like it, suggest that it's enough to imply that a behavior is common if you want others to follow suit.

In fact, this subtle version of social proof is often more powerful than explicitly stating your popularity. Look at the results in Keizer's study: there was a more than doubling of littering when the social norm changed. That's a far bigger effect than in the HMRC tax study.

This is because implying popularity removes some of the skepticism associated with the direct claims of an interested party. If you tell your audience that you're popular, it will have an effect; but this will be tempered by the knowledge that, of course, "that's what you would say." But by creating the impression of popularity and allowing customers to come to their own conclusion, their suspicions will be erased — because they can trust their own judgment, can't they?

But what if you don't have a distinctive color? Is implied social proof something that only certain brands can apply? Not at all. It just requires you to come up with lateral ways to use it.

Behavioral residue

Think about emails. It used to be that you had no idea which device they were being sent from. However, Apple changed that by adding "Sent from my iPhone" to the bottom of emails coming from their smartphones. Recipients soon became aware of how many people owned an iPhone. In contrast, ownership of a Motorola or a Samsung was hidden. Apple felt like the market leader long before it actually was, setting in motion a virtuous circle of social proof.

So, if the purchase or use of your product is invisible, you need to find ways to make it visible.

In his excellent book *Contagious*, Jonah Berger covers many ways brands have made their private consumption more public. But he also talks about the need to leave what he calls "behavioral residue."

Berger notes that the consumption of many products is fleeting. To address this, he argues that brands should consider ways of leaving traces.

In the case of Aperol, the trace is left in the form of their distinctive branded glassware. The glasses have a unique look — they're the exact shape of the bottle neck, turned upside down. So, even when you've finished your cocktail, as long as the glass is on your table, it's clear what you've been drinking.

But you can leave a trace reasonably simply in many other settings. Consider voting in elections. The principle of social proof suggests that if we are aware many people have already voted, we're more likely to do so ourselves. The problem is that once someone has walked out of a voting booth and back on to the street, it's unclear whether they've voted or not. But, pop a little sticker on their jackets and then, long after the event, their voting status remains apparent. And the more stickers are spotted out and about, the more likely it is that citizens will vote.

CHAPTER 6: APEROL

Subtle boasting

Once you recognize the value of hinting at popularity to harness social proof, you'll see that the chances to do so abound.

Here's one idea for you: take the sting out of a potential logistics problem. Running out of stock is obviously a pitfall to be avoided — but if it happens, you can turn it to your advantage. Because if your product has sold out, that's a sure sign that shoppers love it. And what better way to illustrate social proof?

In a 2019 study, Robert Peterson of the University of Texas looked at exactly this challenge. He showed 1,117 participants a product page on a website, with a product labeled as either: "Out of Stock," "Sold Out," or "Unavailable."

Table 5: The term "Sold Out" effectively implies social proof

LABEL	DISAPPOINTMENT WITH PRODUCT	DISAPPOINTMENT WITH WEBSITE
Unavailable	3.48	2.83
Out of Stock	3.61	2.72
Sold Out	3.33	2.41

-15%

Source: Peterson (2019).

Results showed that the term "Sold Out" produced significantly fewer negative reactions than the other two labels. Respondents felt 8% less disappointed with the missing product compared to when it was framed as "Out of Stock." They also felt 15% less disappointed with the overall website compared to when the product was framed as "Unavailable."

Why is this the case? Well, if you use a term like "Unavailable" you're drawing attention to your logistical mistakes. But if you use the phrase, "Sold Out," you're emphasizing the popularity of the item and that draws on social proof.

Simple switches in how a lack of stock is framed can reduce frustration among shoppers, allowing you to leverage the social proof of selling beyond your supply.

The eyes have it

There are other ways to hint at your popularity without making direct claims.

At its heart, social proof is about copying what others are doing. And the behavior we copy can be as understated as the direction of a gaze. You may have noticed it yourself: a small group of observers stop to look at something. Even if the object of their attention is unclear, a crowd soon grows.

So, one subtle effect of social proof is that our eyes are drawn to where others are looking. And that's a fact you can capitalize on in your ads.

The qualitative researcher James Breeze provided evidence of this phenomenon in 2014. He explored how faces can be used to guide readers' attention. He showed 106 participants some ads, which all included images of people. In some cases, the people were looking at the accompanying text (averted gaze); in others, they were looking out at the reader (mutual gaze).

He monitored where readers' attention was drawn using eye-tracking. In Figures 4 and 5, the shaded patches are those areas that attracted attention. The areas bounded by pale halos show the highest attention levels. As expected, a human face always drew attention — especially if it was a baby.

But the surprising finding was that significantly more people read the text when the baby's gaze was fixed on the words than when the baby was looking at the viewer.

Figure 2: A mutual gaze can distract the reader from the key messages

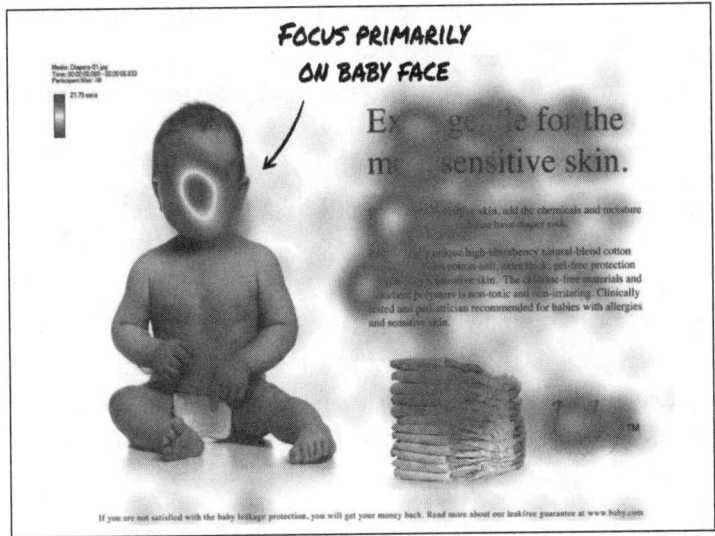

Source: Breeze (2014).

Figure 3: An averted gaze can steer attention to the right spot

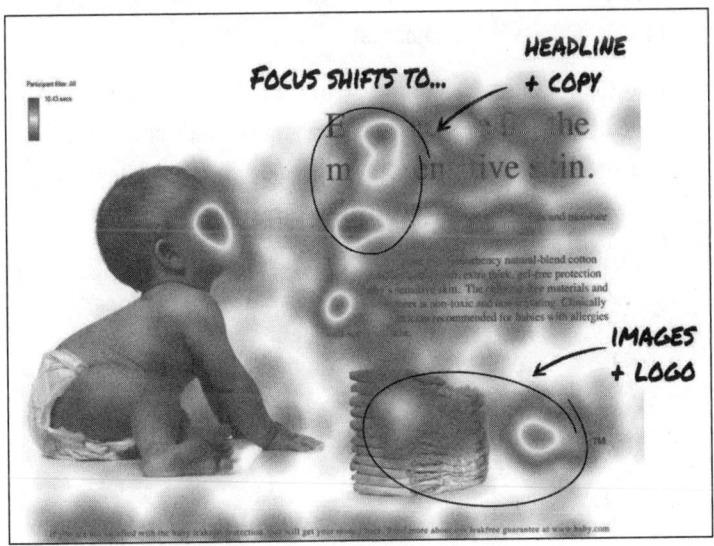

Source: Breeze (2014).

This is a simple trick that you can use to direct customers' attention. If you feature a person in your ad, consider where they're looking. If you want the viewer to read a particular passage, direct the model's gaze towards that text.

Just one more subtle way to harness social proof to your advantage.

THREE KEY TAKEAWAYS

1. **Make your brand visible**: Humans are social animals. We're deeply interested in what others are doing. Make sure the consumption or purchase of your product is as visible as possible. How can you make your product as distinctive and recognizable as Aperol?

2. **Leave a trace**: If you're selling an experience, think about Berger's idea of behavioral residue. Make sure you create a more lasting way for people to broadcast what they have done with your brand. That doesn't have to be complicated. It could be as simple as a voting center handing out stickers.

3. **Point buyers in the right direction**: We're influenced by behaviors as small as a gaze direction. When creating ads, make sure the people in the ads are looking where you want the reader to direct their attention.

7

HÄAGEN-DAZS

WHERE DO YOU think Häagen-Dazs originated? Maybe you've never given it any thought. But if you had to guess, what would you say?

The Netherlands? Germany? Denmark maybe?

You might be surprised to learn that it has nothing to do with any European country — in fact, it hails from the Bronx. And there's a reason for this, grounded in behavioral science.

When life gives you lemons...

Häagen-Dazs was created by Reuben Mattus, who arrived in New York in 1921 aged nine, and was put to work squeezing lemons for his uncle's Italian ice business.

The company did well, but by the 1950s the ice cream market was becoming crowded. So, Mattus and his wife, Rose, decided to develop a new product that would set them apart: a superior ice cream aimed at people looking for luxury. Made of richer, heavier, more premium ingredients, the first high-end ice cream was launched in 1960.

Mattus was astute enough to know that a great product wasn't enough. With a natural flair for marketing, he opted for a price point that would reflect the luxury of the product — 75 cents a pint, 30% more than the competition at 52 cents.[19]

But this wasn't his only marketing ploy. In a 1990 interview with journalist Joan Nathan, he said:

> The most important thing was to make it taste good. The second most important thing was to market it properly. I prided myself on being a marketing man. If you're the same like everybody else, you're lost. The number one thing was to get a foreign sounding name.[20]

The genesis of a name

Reuben and Rose decided that a foreign name would help the brand stand out. But they also wanted to benefit from the associated value of exotic, exciting otherness.

To achieve this, they chose a country which, in 1960s America, captured these positive associations. It could have been one of many European nations. But they selected Denmark since it was, according to Mattus, "[t]he only country which saved the Jews during World War II."

The couple then brainstormed hundreds of words that sounded Danish, to their American ears, until they hit on Häagen-Dazs.

Just to be sure that shoppers picked up on the supposed Scandinavian roots, they added an umlaut over the "a" and put a map of Denmark on the packaging. While this may have fooled customers, it's worth noting that umlauts appear in Swedish but not Danish. And the "zs" ending only appears in Hungarian. As

Reuben recalled, "I put together a totally fictitious Danish name and had it registered."

Their trick worked. The brand spread rapidly by word of mouth. By 1973, Häagen-Dazs was stocked nationally; and soon the company had launched "scoop shops."

By 1983, Häagen-Dazs had become so successful that Pillsbury bought it for $70 million (that's the equivalent of $221 million today).[21] Ownership has changed many times since then — the company is now owned by General Mills and is still one of the most successful ice cream brands in the world.

What can we learn from Häagen-Dazs?

The most striking point about the Häagen-Dazs story is the adoption of foreign branding. In this case, the brand sought to benefit from the favorable associations that Denmark held in American consumers' minds as a sophisticated and admirable country.

There's evidence that associations based on provenance boost the probability people will try a brand — and, perhaps more surprisingly, will boost enjoyment of the product too.

One such study comes from the world of wine. In 2007, two professors from Cornell University, Brian Wansink and Collin Payne, and assistant professor Jill North from the University of Illinois, explored how the perceived provenance of wine can influence its taste.[22]

The psychologists served diners the same cabernet sauvignon. However, sometimes the bottles were labeled as being from North Dakota, and other times California. Participants who drank the "Californian" wine rated it 41% higher than the "North Dakota" group.

As we discussed in the chapter on Kraft, what we experience is affected by what we expect to experience. If you set up a positive set of expectations for your product it won't just increase trial, it will boost the actual enjoyment.

This isn't a one-off result. For example, in 2014, Ali Kara at Pennsylvania State University carried out a study of 3,373 shoppers at malls in 17 Turkish cities. Participants were asked to look at a print ad for a product from one of two well-known brands: Adidas, a German brand (sneakers or a purse); and Philips, a Dutch brand (a TV or kettle).

The twist was that some participants were told the product had been made in China, rather than Germany/the Netherlands. Respondents then indicated their trust in the brand, perceptions of quality, and purchase intentions.

Kara found that when the products apparently came from China, customer perceptions on all three metrics were lower than when the products were supposedly manufactured in the Netherlands or Germany.

Another study looked specifically at Häagen-Dazs. In 2017, Thomas Aichner, an assistant professor of marketing at the University of Padova in Italy, investigated the "Häagen-Dazs effect." He informed customers in a German supermarket that Häagen-Dazs is not, in fact, Danish at all, but rather a hearty Bronx product. The result? Willingness to buy Häagen-Dazs products dropped 68%.

So, foreign branding works. Or at least, it works if you build an association with a country that exemplifies the attributes you want to convey.

Foreign-branded products

Foreign branding is distinct from genuine foreign products. One example of the latter is Fjällräven, a Swedish outdoor clothing brand named after the word for "arctic fox" in Swedish, which has succeeded globally.

CHAPTER 7: HÄAGEN-DAZS

However, foreign branding is a common tactic. Superdry is Japanese, right? Nope. Made in Cheltenham, UK.

Once you start digging, you'll see that foreign branding is surprisingly common.* Here are a few more examples…

Atari

This gaming brand, responsible for smash hits in arcade games as well as home consoles, rose to peak popularity in the 1980s and 1990s. The word *"Atari"* — Japanese for "to hit a target"— conjures images of futuristic electronics. But guess what? It's a brand born and raised in Sunnyvale, California.

Berghaus

This is a premium outdoor brand that's synonymous with quality. These sound like German traits, and the name is a German-sounding word. But no: Berghaus was invented by two Brits, Peter Lockey and Gordon Davison, in Northeast England.

Both keen climbers, they began with an outdoor store called LD (Lockey Davison) Mountain Centre, before introducing their own brand of kit and naming it after the German translation of their store: "mountain house." It was a deliberate move because at the time, German engineering was associated with reliability and performance.

Starbucks

It doesn't have to be the brand name that's foreign to benefit from positive associations. Think about Starbucks. It's not the name that sounds foreign, but the drinks. Most of the labels we now associate with coffees — espresso, macchiato, Americano — are Italian. And this is not unique to Starbucks.

But following a trip to Italy, CEO Howard Schultz took this a

---

* Even the British Royal Family tapped into the principle: in 1917, at the height of World War I, they changed their name. At that point, they were the House of Saxe-Coburg-Gotha. But anti-German sentiment was rampant in Britain, and it seemed wise to adopt something more English-sounding — hence, the House of Windsor.

step further and applied the practice to other elements, like sizing: Venti, Grande, Trenta.[23] As Karen Blumenthal wrote in her book, *Grande Expectations*, Schultz "wanted to convey a different image, something far more exotic than a simple cup of joe." And "since the stores were designed around the concept of Italian coffee bars, [Schultz] wanted distinctive names."

Accepting deceit?

You may have ethical concerns about this approach. Perhaps in the 1960s, as a then-small, local company operating out of the Bronx, it could be seen as excusable — maybe even charming — for Häagen-Dazs to do this. But is such subterfuge still acceptable today? Could launching a fake foreign brand look like a cynical attempt to appropriate the culture of others and deceive the public?

Possibly. As Aichner's experiment above shows, when customers uncover the truth, they may not be too happy with you. In the long term, if your Machiavellian ways are discovered, your brand could suffer.

We recommend that marketers maintain high moral standards. Just because a tactic can influence consumers doesn't mean you should use it. If you exploit customers' psychology through obvious deceit, you may benefit from a short-term boost in sales at the cost of long-term brand image.

Even so, studying the Häagen-Dazs example teaches us a lot. For one, when applying the findings of academic studies, there is always an element of nuance involved. Context is important. For example, Starbucks' naming system feels acceptable to us because we've already happily adopted Italian nomenclature for our coffee.

But how do you identify how much "fake" foreign branding is too much? A good principle to abide by is one suggested by philosopher John Rawls, and highlighted by Richard Thaler in *Nudge*, called the *publicity principle*. In simplified terms, the argument is that organizations should never develop policies that they'd be unwilling to defend in public. This is useful advice for a brand: if it's something you'd be embarrassed about, don't do it.

Mightier than the sword

If the foreign branding technique doesn't seem right for your brand, what else could you try?

Well, foreign branding is just one way of using descriptive language to influence how customers interpret things. Choice of words is crucial. This point is demonstrated in a classic study from 1974 by Elizabeth Loftus and John Palmer at the University of Washington.

But before reading about the study, if you can, go to YouTube and search for "Loftus and Palmer Replication Crash Footage."

It's a clip of a car crash, which Loftus and Palmer showed to participants in their study. After watching the film, participants were asked to estimate how fast the cars were moving when the accident occurred.

However, the verb in the question was changed between participants. Specifically, each was asked: "About how fast were the cars going when they [smashed/collided/bumped/hit/contacted] each other?"

The choice of verb had a significant impact on speed estimations. Participants who were asked about when the cars "smashed" thought the vehicles were traveling 27% faster than those who were asked the "contacted" question.

The psychologists ran the study five times in total, each time varying the verb used and each time receiving distinctly different speed estimates.

You can see the full results in the table.

Table 6: The label used to describe an event affects its interpretation

VERB	SPEED ESTIMATE (MPH)
Smashed	40.5
Collided	39.3
Bumped	38.1
Hit	34.0
Contacted	31.8

+27%

Source: Adapted from Loftus and Palmer (1974).

The point of Loftus and Palmer's study is that people don't interpret events neutrally. In fact, that's why the pair conducted the study: they wanted to demonstrate that the words used when police question a witness can impact their testimony.

The results show clearly that language acts as a lens, altering our interpretation. Your job as a marketer is to pick the language that creates the most positive interpretation.

A fish by any other name...

The tale of the popular Chilean sea bass is an excellent illustration of the power of names.

In the late 1970s, American fish importer Lee Lantz tried to encourage restaurants to add a new dish to their menus: the Patagonian toothfish.

Although tasty, the dish wasn't proving popular. Perhaps, thought Lantz, the name was putting restaurateurs off. So, drawing on the work of Loftus, he came up with an alternative — the Chilean sea bass. It was only after relabeling the fish that sales began to boom:

CHAPTER 7: HÄAGEN-DAZS

there was a 30-fold increase in consumption of sea bass during the 1990s alone,[24] and it remains a popular dish today. So popular, in fact, that authorities have had to regulate the numbers caught in order to sustain the population.

The naming of fish, it turns out, offers marketers a masterclass in the importance of language. Would you order dolphin fish? Probably not, as it conjures images of Flipper — everyone's favorite marine animal. Rebranded as mahi mahi, though, the dish sounds more acceptable. Or, anyone for mudbug linguine? Thought not. But rename it as crawfish and *voilà* — sounds delicious! There are plenty more examples to choose from.

These fishy tales might sound like a special case. But the idea that the label you choose can strongly shape how people perceive your product has far-reaching implications.

> The label you choose can strongly shape how people perceive your product.

Imagine you're a politician and you want to persuade people that inheritance tax should be increased. It would be easy to focus on a logical argument. But that would do your case a disservice, because the label is just as important. If you call the tax an "estate tax," this sounds like something people could get on board with. Whereas if you label it a "death tax," you'll dampen support.

The swing occurs because each phrase conjures up a different set of images: "estate tax" insinuates that it's the wealthy 1% who'll pay. "Death tax" emphasizes that the money will be collected at the most insensitive time, when you're in the throes of grief.

This isn't speculation. Pollster Frank Luntz reports that 68% of people oppose inheritance tax if it's labelled "estate tax," but the figure jumps to 78% when it's called a "death tax."

Or, moving from the realm of politics to the commercial world, imagine you run a travel website that charges a booking fee. The Loftus and Palmer study suggests that by altering your language, you can change people's willingness to pay. For example, switch from calling it a "booking fee" to a "service cost." The word "service" emphasizes the efforts that you have expended in creating the offering. And the word "cost" conveys a more neutral covering of expenses, whereas "fee" insinuates a markup.

Finally, imagine you run a restaurant. If you want to sell a vegetarian dish, it's better to label it "field grown" than "meat free." The former, by drawing on the provenance of the dish, highlights its appeal; whereas the latter calls attention to what's not in the dish, making it feel like something's missing.

If you develop a great product and expect it to be judged on its inherent attributes alone, you're in for a rude awakening. You need to spend as much time on picking the right label as you do finessing the underlying offering.

THREE KEY TAKEAWAYS

1. **Expectations shape experiences**: We experience, to a degree, what we expect to experience. If you want to maximize appreciation of your product, it's not enough to have a wonderful product — use language to create a positive set of expectations around it too.

2. **Nudge ethically**: Just because a bias exists, doesn't mean you should use it. Apply your own judgment to work out which nudges go too far. If you're not happy defending your decision in public, don't go there.

3. **Choose your words carefully**: Be careful about the words you choose. Sometimes they can have unexpected effects. For example, if you associate your brand with a particular country, customers will project their perceptions of that country onto your products.

8

RED BULL

TRUCK DRIVERS IN 1970s Thailand used to rely on a caffeine-heavy soft drink to keep them on the road. How did we get from that to the global energy drink leader that we know today? Some behavioral biases lent a hand.

From wheels to wings

In 1975, Krating Daeng — a non-carbonated blend of caffeine, sugar, taurine, and B-vitamins — was a favorite among Thai workers. It gave them the energy to power through gruelling, long shifts.

But it wasn't until an Austrian named Dietrich Mateschitz came across it that the drink took flight globally. On a trip to Thailand in 1982, he was recommended it as a remedy for jetlag — and it worked.

Mateschitz was employed by a German toothpaste manufacturer at the time, but he was an entrepreneur at heart. In a business meeting with the owner of a small pharma company, he learned that he was talking to Chaleo Yoovidhya — the maker of the amazing drink that had given him a lift that day. He was struck by the opportunity. Why not, he suggested, adapt the energy drink for a worldwide market?

Yoovidhya jumped at the chance. Together they adapted the recipe for a slightly different palate — a process that took three years — and called it Red Bull. A whole new category of beverage was born in the West, with the first European launch in Austria. Soon the slogan "Red Bull Gives you Wings" was helping the brand to take off all over the world.

Since its introduction in 1987, Red Bull has expanded its distribution to more than 171 countries and sold over 12 billion cans in 2023 alone.[25] It's now the world's most-consumed energy drink.

A can to defy comparison

As well as its energy-promoting properties, Red Bull has another clear distinguishing feature: the can. At the time of its launch, soft drinks were invariably sold in 12oz (355ml) cans measuring about 12cm tall and 6cm wide. But Mateschitz decided to switch things up, and the brand launched with taller, slimmer cans, holding 8.45oz (250ml) and measuring 14cm by 4cm. Red Bull was the first drink to appear in this size.

By offering a totally new can size, Red Bull made it clear from the start that this was not your average soda. This approach gave the brand leeway with its pricing.

Opting for a different shape removed the comparator group. And comparison is very important: we tend to judge value in relation to other prices — it's called *price relativity*. Having nothing to benchmark against makes it hard for buyers to gauge whether a product offers good value.

There's good real-world evidence to support this assertion. In 2022, we carried out our own research 404 shoppers. We told

CHAPTER 8: RED BULL

everyone that a 16oz tub of Ben & Jerry's ice cream cost $3.99 and then asked them how good-value they thought it was.

The twist was that half of the respondents were also told that the same weight of Walmart's own-label ice cream cost just $1.99. Of that group, only 27% thought Ben & Jerry's was great value.

The other half of the respondents saw the same Ben & Jerry's tub, still priced at $3.99 for 16 oz. But this time, they were shown an equal-sized Halo Top tub alongside, priced at a costlier $4.99. In this set-up, many more people — in fact, 41% — thought Ben & Jerry's represented great value. That's a 52% difference.

Table 7: We judge value relatively, not absolutely

BEN & JERRY'S PRICE	COMPARISON PRICE	PROPORTION THINKING BEN & JERRY'S WAS GOOD OR GREAT VALUE
$3.99	$1.99 (Walmart Owned Label)	27%
$3.99	$4.99 (Halo Top)	41%

+52%

Source: Shotton and Flicker (2022).

These findings show that we judge price in relative, not absolute, terms. The same figure can appear to offer great value or not, depending on what we compare it with.

When Red Bull first hit the stores, its first-of-a-kind can size made it difficult for shoppers to check the price against other sodas. Customers were all at sea, with no other figure to latch onto. So Red Bull was at liberty to push the pricing. Which is one of the reasons why a can will set you back around $2.50 — versus around $1 for a can of Coca-Cola.

Playing with size

It might feel like a stretch to claim that such a subtle shift in size and shape can influence drinkers. But Richard ran a test exploring this very tactic, looking at beer.

King Cobra is a high-strength lager available in the UK and served in larger-than-average glass bottles — 750ml, the same as a wine bottle. He showed this beer alongside half a dozen other drinks to participants* and asked them how much they would be prepared to pay for it in a superstore.

In the first test, King Cobra was shown alongside other bottled beers. In this scenario, participants were prepared to pay £3.75 ($4.90). In a second test, King Cobra was presented alongside a selection of wines. This time, participants suggested a price of £4.80 ($6.27) — that's 28% more.

The comparison group had a significant impact on participants' willingness to pay. The surrounding drinks set a benchmark: a bottled beer sets a benchmark of a couple of pounds, whereas a bottle of wine establishes a higher one.

This is good evidence to support Red Bull's decision to remove standard sodas as a comparison set. Shoppers would have viewed the drinks directly alongside standard-sized drinks cans and may well have considered the price of Red Bull to be excessive in comparison.

As Vice Chairman of Ogilvy, UK, and author Rory Sutherland says in his book *Alchemy*:

> How can Red Bull charge £1.50 a can when Coke only charges 50p? Weirdly you make the can smaller. Suddenly people think this is a different category of drink for which

---

* The participants weren't nationally representative so take these findings as indicative.

different price points apply. If the can had been the same size, I am not sure they could have charged £1.50. Logic won't tell you that and research won't tell you, because in research we all pretend we are maximisers and hyper-rational.

Going global

Behavioral science doubters sometimes question whether the findings from psychological studies are applicable outside of the Western settings in which they are generally conducted. And this is a valid consideration. Of course, re-testing and replication should be ongoing, and bodies of research continue to expand in new settings. But there are some biases that have already been shown to hold true in various countries — including findings about the significance of price relativity.

For example, Richard also conducted price relativity experiments with an Indian audience. This time, he showed participants a 100g box of Tata Tea priced at 483 rupees, alongside a box of Brooke Bond tea of the same weight priced at 292 rupees. In this scenario, when asked whether Tata Tea was good value, 65% of participants agreed.

Next, he asked a different group the same question, but this time compared Tata Tea to a 100g box of Lipton priced at a more costly 966 rupees. In this scenario, 80% of participants thought Tata Tea was good value — a difference of 23% versus the comparison with Brooke Bond. The results are shown in Table 8.

Table 8: Price relativity is not just a Western construct

TATA TEA PRICE (RUPEES)	COMPARISON PRICE (RUPEES)	PROPORTION THINKING TATA TEA WAS GOOD OR GREAT VALUE
483	292 (Brooke Bond)	65%
483	966 (Lipton)	80%

+23%

Source: Shotton (2020).

For a global brand like Red Bull, this is significant. Knowing that shoppers worldwide will decide whether to buy based on the comparison set for Red Bull means that choosing an unusual can size is likely to be effective in many markets — and could in part explain the brand's global success.

Certainly, it's a tactic that's been put to good use by other brands. A lovely example comes from Bell cycle helmets. In one ad, it encourages parents to compare the price of its life-saving safety helmet with the price of a pair of sneakers. The headline reads: "Does your kid have hundred dollar feet and a ten dollar head?"

The helmet was a high-spec version, at the costlier end of the spectrum. Without a comparator, parents would naturally weigh it up versus other, cheaper cycle helmets. But framing it against sneakers changed that. Compared with the latest footwear styles, the cost of the helmet feels low. What parent would put more value on fashion than their child's life?

Another wonderfully creative example comes from German train company Deutsche Bahn, whose task was to encourage folks to holiday at home rather than travel abroad.

In 2019, using Facebook data, it identified people researching foreign trips and showed them an image of a tourist attraction in that destination. For example, someone considering traveling to Arizona would see a picture of the Horseshoe Bend on the

Colorado River accompanied by the relevant airfare, which was roughly €1,100.

Then, in real time, Deutsche Bahn scraped the Getty Images database and found what it called a doppelganger site: a tourist attraction at home in Germany that looked remarkably similar. In this case, the Moselle Bend at Bremm. It then accompanied that image with the rail fare to get there: €19.

This brilliantly applies price relativity.

Think what most marketers would have done. The obvious way to encourage Germans to holiday at home would be to show them images of beautiful local sights and tell them the train fare.

But that tactic leaves the comparison set unstated. And, left to their own devices, people are likely to compare the rail fare to a tank of petrol. In that case, €19 only looks like reasonable value.

But if you introduce the comparison of a transatlantic airline ticket, suddenly €19 looks like a rounding error. The appeal of exactly the same price varies according to what it's compared to.

A badge of quality

Removing the standard drinks can comparison opened the door for Red Bull to play with pricing, and by opting for the higher end, the brand successfully harnessed another hardwired mental shortcut: *price as a badge of quality*.

As we've seen, people tend to experience what they expect to experience. Price is one factor that significantly informs not only our expectations, but also our actual enjoyment of a product.

> **People tend to experience what they expect to experience.**

Evidence of this comes from research conducted in 2008 by Hilke Plassmann of the California Institute of Technology and

Baba Shiv of Stanford University, who explored the impact of price on wine evaluation.

In this study, participants were asked to taste several wines and rate how much they liked them on a scale from one to six (one = not at all; six = very much). What they did not know is that two of the wines were the same but had been labeled with different prices: $45 and $5.

Even though they were the same drink, participants rated the apparently expensive wine 70% higher than the wine labeled at a low price.

The results clearly show the extent to which price guides our perceptions. And this doesn't only apply to wine: David Just, a behavioral economist at Cornell University, has looked at pizza; Richard has run his own tests with perfume and, most pertinently, Baba Shiv has conducted a study with energy drinks. The findings remain consistent. The higher the price, the more we like a product.

So, stamping that higher price bracket onto Red Bull means we'll like it more than if it was cheaper. And so, we come back for more.

Costly signaling

The final bias that Red Bull applied is another one that relates to money: *costly signaling*. This theory suggests that consumers take high advertising spends as a signal of self-confidence. It probably has roots in biology, where animals that can afford costly displays — such as peacock feathers — signal their fitness as potential mates.

The original evidence comes from a study by Amna Kirmani at Duke University and Peter Wright at Stanford University. In 1989, they tested the extent to which high ad spend acts as a costly signal.

They gave 214 participants a magazine article describing the launch of a new sneaker. The article included the amount the brand spent on its campaign: there were four versions of the article, citing spends of $2 million, $10 million, $20 million, or $40 million.

As context, the piece also referred to the sum that global athletic brands such as Nike and New Balance would typically spend on a new product launch — around $10 million.

Participants were asked to indicate the quality of the shoe on a nine-point scale (one = much lower than average; nine = much higher than average). The mean results for each group are shown in Table 9.

Table 9: Higher perceived ad spend results in higher perceived quality

REPORTED COST OF CAMPAIGN	PERCEIVED QUALITY
$2 million	5.39
$10 million	5.67
$20 million	6.16
$40 million	5.71

+14% (between $2 million and $20 million)

Source: Adapted from Kirmani and Wright (1989).

As you can see, perceived quality increases with reported spend — a $20 million spend resulted in a 14% higher perceived quality than a $2 million spend.

The psychologists' argument was that an extravagant spend acts as a screening mechanism. Since flamboyant advertising only pays off in the long term, a brand would need to have a genuine belief in the product to be confident in making that investment.

However, there was a limit to this. When spend was deemed excessive ($40 million), quality ratings were only slightly higher than the lowest spend levels. In this extreme case, perhaps people worry that the excessive spend on advertising is an act of desperation.

In the Kirmani study, participants were explicitly told the ad spend of the brand. That's slightly unrealistic.

So Thinkbox, the body that promotes TV advertising in the UK, investigated whether more subtle cues could be used for costly signaling — and, particularly, whether the choice of medium could affect brand perceptions.[26] After all, there's a significant difference between the cost of a TV campaign and a social media campaign.

Thinkbox showed 3,600 people a description of an imaginary brand called TIXE. The brand name was used to describe one of four products: an online retailer, a detergent, a cellphone network, or home insurance.

Respondents were given a brief outline of a brand's launch advertising campaign. All information was identical except the medium being used. For each participant, this was listed as one of the following: TV, newspapers, magazines, radio, social media, or video sharing sites.

Through implicit and explicit questioning, Thinkbox gauged the effect of the media channel on respondents' perceptions of the brand, focusing on factors such as quality, financial strength, popularity, success, and trustworthiness.

They found that TV ads drove the strongest responses across all metrics. For example, 43% rated the brand as high quality when it used TV, compared to just 19% when it used social media. On average, the scores were 47% for TV and 28% for social media, with newspapers, magazines, and radio somewhere in the middle (37%, 38%, and 39%, respectively).

So, TV boosts quality and trust perceptions. But why? One explanation is that viewers are aware that it's the most expensive form of advertising. This offers further support for the idea that obviously higher expenditure by a brand will serve it well in the eyes of customers.

CHAPTER 8: RED BULL

And Red Bull is nothing if not extravagant in its marketing. In fact, it's a master of experiential marketing. In a 2002 interview for *The Economist*, Mateschitz said: "We don't bring the product to the people, we bring people to the product."[27]

Quirky events launched by Red Bull, like the Flugtag amateur flying machine contest, have gained the brand international attention. Then came sponsorship of football teams; and now we have Red Bull F1. These deals cost the company — but boy, do they signal confidence.

Perhaps none of these initiatives have been as audacious as the Red Bull Stratos space jump, in which high-altitude skydiver Felix Baumgartner flew in a helium balloon 24 miles into the stratosphere and then freefell back to Earth. His descent lasted approximately ten minutes, and broke world skydiving records, as well as the sound barrier — he reached an unimaginable terminal velocity of almost 844 miles per hour.[28] Amazingly, Felix landed safely on his feet.

The stunt was livestreamed and viewed by more than 9.5 million people.[29] Now, this astonishing feat didn't come cheap. Hundreds of personnel were involved — not to mention the cutting-edge gear designed to withstand conditions at the edge of space. One estimate put the price tag at $30 million.[30] Every person who heard about it would have been aware of the immense cost to Red Bull, whose logo was emblazoned on Felix's helmet and suit, and the capsule he leapt out of.

The stunt demonstrated huge brand confidence, which translated into consumer confidence. It resulted in a significant boost in sales — reportedly as much as $500 million.[31] Success on every front.

The audacity of Red Bull Stratos signaled supreme brand self-belief which, coupled with the almost-but-not-quite unacceptable cost of the drink, helped Red Bull to be perceived as a highly successful premium energy drink.

THREE KEY TAKEAWAYS

1. **Change your comparison set**: Establish the mental comparison set for your product and you can change your customers' willingness to pay by orders of magnitude. Prices are viewed relatively rather than absolutely. A product sold at the same price can be viewed as either good value or bad value, depending on what that item is being compared to. This creates tremendous opportunity for a creative marketer.

2. **Use price to signal quality**: The price you charge will set quality expectations. People assume that expensive products are superior to cheaper ones and these expectations affect the actual experience of the product. Be careful about excessive promotions because you risk training your shopper to think your product is low quality.

3. **Spend big to look believable**: Consider an extravagant display of advertising to persuade a skeptical audience. People are far more likely to believe a message if they think the brand has spent heavily on its communications. After all, only a company with genuine faith in its product would invest for the long term.

9

GUINNESS

THE GUINNESS BRAND is over 260 years old, but their ads have only been running for 90 years.

Having waited 170 years for the ads to arrive we should perhaps have expected superior quality. After all, good things come to those who wait — and that's exactly what lies at the heart of the brand.

Exceptional quality

In 1759, Arthur Guinness took out a 9,000-year lease on St James' Gate brewery in Dublin, Ireland. That's how confident he was of future success. And his confidence was well placed. Ten years later, he began exporting to Great Britain and today the brand is now available in 150 countries.[32]

Key to Guinness' success has been a deeply embedded focus on exellence. In fact, no matter where it's brewed or served, every pint, bottle or can of Guinness must adhere to a set of strict standards. It is said that every barrel undergoes up to 400 quality checks, including 23 taste tests.[33]

This focus on quality carries through to the ads. Up until 1929, Guinness didn't advertise — the family let the product speak for itself. They were finally persuaded to start advertising on condition that the ads would be as high caliber as the stout.

And they started strong. The first campaign featured the now-famous "Guinness is good for you" slogan, penned by novelist (and natural copywriter) Dorothy L. Sayers. Classic artwork came from John Gilroy.

Since then, Guinness advertising has earned cult status. That success has been driven by the company's relentless quest for ever better advertising. So, in 1997, even though its last campaign had been reasonably successful, it came as no surprise when Guinness put the account up for pitch.

The brief sent out to agencies included one interesting stipulation: under no circumstances should the campaign talk about the stout's slow pour. The aim was to win over lager drinkers and the brand was concerned the wait might put them off.

Anticipation is all

One of the agencies asked to pitch was Abbott Mead Vickers (AMV).

Thankfully, AMV creative Walter Campbell wasn't always a strict rule-follower. He'd come to the pitch a week late, with his boss — legendary copywriter David Abbott — believing he'd be too busy to take it on. But overnight, a few thoughts came to him, including reviving the original concept of "goodness" from the first-ever Guinness ads ("Guinness is good for you"), and ideas around the passage of time. He went back to the brief and carefully ignored its stipulations.

Why? Because he'd noticed from his friends' drinking behavior that they seemed to like things done properly, and that the wait was an important part of getting a good pint. He decided that, rather than putting drinkers off, the length of time taken during pouring was one of the brand's big draws. It served to fuel the anticipatory joy of the night ahead.

Combining this sense of anticipation with the idea that Guinness is good, he came up with: "Good things come to those who wait." It won AMV the pitch, and the new campaign launched with Campbell's "Swim Black" ad. It's a story crafted around Guinness's slow pour, with the time it takes to pour the perfect pint — 119.5 seconds, to be precise — signaling quality and credibility.[34]

This ad was followed by the famous "Surfer" in 1999, depicting a surfer gazing intently and patiently out to sea, trying to spot the perfect wave before plunging into the water. As in the 1998 ad, the "Good things come to those who wait" message appeared at the end of "Surfer" along with the voiceover words, "Here's to waiting."[35]

The results were impressive: the campaign, according to Campbell, was credited with a 12% increase in Guinness sales.[36]

The idea was reprised in a 2020 US TV commercial featuring quarterback legend Joe Montana and the famous Superbowl touchdown that had fans waiting on the edges of their seats.[37]

What's going on?

It takes a long time to pour a good pint of Guinness: almost two minutes, if the ads are to be believed. Now, if you and your pals have ordered drinks at the bar together and your friends are already happily sipping while you're still waiting for your pint, this delay could be considered a downside.

Broadcasting this fact in your commercials might thus seem counterintuitive. But in choosing to admit this flaw, Guinness is harnessing a well-known, but underused, bias called the *pratfall effect*.

Essentially, this predicts that we find people who admit flaws more appealing. Evidence of the power of this bias comes from a classic experiment by Harvard psychologist Elliot Aronson.

In 1966, he set out to explore how small blunders might change how we feel about a person. First, he recorded an actor answering a series of quiz questions. In his initial experiment, the actor had been prepped with the correct answers, so was able to score 92%. After the quiz, the actor pretended to spill a cup of coffee over himself (a small blunder, or pratfall).

> We find people who admit flaws more appealing.

An audio recording of the quiz was then played to the study participants, who were asked to rate how much they liked the contestant.

However, Aronson split the sample into two groups. One group heard the entire recording, spillage and all, while the other heard it with the blunder edited out.

Results showed that the participants preferred the contestant if they heard him spill his coffee — in fact, they found the clumsy contestant 45% more likable.

Extrapolating from person to brand, we can conclude that those which admit a flaw will boost their appeal. And this is what Guinness is doing in its ads: by admitting how long it takes to pour a pint, the company taps into the pratfall effect. As AMV creative Campbell told us: "There's something beautiful in the fallibility of a thing."

It's not just Guinness that has leveraged this idea. If you look at the greatest-ever ads, it's remarkable how often the pratfall effect is used.

Think about the classic VW ads with lines such as, "Ugly is only skin-deep," "Lemon," or "America's slowest fastback."

Or Avis: "When you're only No. 2, you try harder."

Or Listerine: "The taste people hate. Twice a day."

CHAPTER 9: GUINNESS

Or Southwest Airlines: "We're Not Fancy."

Again and again, the greatest brands boost their appeal by admitting a weakness.

But before you rush to apply this idea, there's a caveat. Aronson showed that a person needs to have a degree of perceived competence to benefit from this effect. In a second setup, he recruited another group of participants and played an audio recording of the contestant failing the quiz, answering just 32% of the questions correctly. As before, half heard a recording including the coffee spill; the other heard it without.

This time around, the results were quite different. Participants rated the not-so-smart quiz contestant who spilled his coffee as *less* likable than the not-so-smart one who didn't make the blunder. This suggests that the pratfall effect is only effective when there's an underlying level of confidence in the person. It backfires if that's missing. You can see the study results in Table 10.

Table 10: Competent people who exhibit a small flaw become more appealing

	ATTRACTION SCORES	
	NO PRATFALL	PRATFALL
SUPERIOR ABILITY	20.8 →	30.2 +45%
AVERAGE ABILITY	17.8 →	-2.5 -114%

Source: Adapted from Aronson (1966).

So, as a brand, be sure your customers have enough confidence in your core offer before admitting a weakness.

Take the wind out of negative sails

But the pratfall effect isn't the only reason why the line "Good things come to those who wait" is so successful. The second role it plays is in bridging the trust gap.

Consumers aren't dumb: they're naturally suspicious. They know that brands have a financial interest in spinning the truth. So, anything you say is likely to be treated skeptically.

That's not a new phenomenon. We're sure if you went back to Ancient Rome, buyers would have been cautious about trusting the olive oil salesman. A sharp shopper would recognize that the merchant's claims of quality had more to do with shifting the stock than a strict reflection of the truth.

So, why does communicating a flaw help overcome this issue? Well, if you admit a meaningful problem, you have tangibly proved your honesty, and then everything else you say becomes that much more believable. It lends the brand credibility.

> If you admit a meaningful problem, you have tangibly proved your honesty, and then everything else you say becomes that much more believable.

The best creatives have long recognized this. Bill Bernbach — founder of DDB, the agency behind the VW and Avis ads, and perhaps the most respected creative director of all time — used to say, "A small admission gains a large acceptance."

Most pertinently to Guinness, AMV founder David Abbott argued that: "Confession is good for the soul and for copy, too."

The intuition of these creative directors is supported by experimental evidence.

In 1993, Kipling Williams and colleagues at the University of

Toledo led a study in a legal setting into what they called the *stolen thunder technique*. This refers to a tactic whereby a defense attorney in court admits a weakness in their case *before* the prosecution has a chance to bring it up.

For his study, Williams recruited 257 participants and asked them to read one of three versions of a criminal assault trial. The accounts were all the same apart from one detail: sometimes a damaging piece of evidence about the defendant was absent (no thunder); sometimes it was brought up by the prosecutor (thunder); and sometimes it was first brought up by the defense (stolen thunder).

Participants were asked whether they thought the defendant was guilty, using an 11-point scale (1 = definitely not guilty; 11 = definitely guilty). You can see the results in Table 11.

Table 11: Admitting a problem before it's raised makes for a better outcome

TRIAL VERSION	PERCEPTIONS OF DEFENDANT'S GUILT
Thunder (prosecution reveals evidence)	6.61
Stolen thunder (defence admits evidence)	5.83
No thunder (evidence is not revealed)	5.04

-12%

Source: Adapted from Williams (1993).

The results show that a defendant is 12% more likely to walk free if any damning evidence is shared by their own side, rather than the prosecution. That's the case even if the attorney does nothing to refute this evidence.

In this study, as you'd expect, it still worked out best for the defendant if the negative story didn't come to light at all. Without that piece of negative evidence — no thunder — participants rated the chance of guilt at 5.04.

But if there's an issue and a real chance it'll be called out, it's far better to admit it up front than wait for people to come to the realization themselves.

It reduces the impact of the negative element and boosts credibility at the same time.

This is exactly the approach taken by Guinness. Customers have to wait. They know they have to wait, so why not just accept that — or even turn it into a selling point?

A positive negative

The real beauty of the Guinness ads, though, lies in the choice of the flaw they flaunt. Because the flipside of their weakness — the long wait — is quality. We naturally equate the length of time it takes to create something with its quality.

There's no corner-cutting when it comes to Guinness. It takes time because the thick, smooth texture of Guinness and the mix of nitrogen and carbon dioxide used to make it froth mean that it takes longer to settle than standard beer.

So really, the slow pour is a key sign of its caliber. When viewed that way, it makes complete sense to highlight it.

Other examples of weakness reframed as strength include Stella Artois "Reassuringly Expensive," where we connect cost with quality. Or Canadian cough syrup Buckley's "It tastes awful. And it works," which relies on natural assumptions about foul flavor equating with a powerful effect.

There's a study that clearly demonstrates the importance of admitting a negative issue that complements your core strength. The experiment, from 2003, comes from Gerd Bohner and colleagues at Bielefeld University in Germany, who investigated the impact of the pratfall effect on attitudes towards a restaurant. The researchers recruited 131 participants and split them into three groups, each shown a different ad for a fictitious Italian eatery called Fresco Francesco:

- Group one were told about only positive features (e.g., cosy atmosphere).
- Group two were shown positive features (e.g., cosy atmosphere) and *unrelated* negative features (e.g., no dedicated parking spaces).
- Group three were shown positive features (e.g., cosy atmosphere) and *related* negative features (e.g., inability to accommodate parties of more than four).

Each participant rated their attitude to the restaurant on a scale of one to nine (one = very bad; nine = very good). Interestingly, the ad with only positive features scored the lowest (4.29). In line with the pratfall effect, there was a slight improvement for the ad including the unrelated negative feature (4.51). But the most successful ad by far was the one with the related negatives (5.62). In that setting, the restaurant was rated 31% better than in the positive-only group.

In many cultures, strengths and weaknesses are two sides of the same coin. Shoppers know from bitter experience that products can't be all things to all people. If you want quality, you tend to have to pay for it. If you want the tastiest burger, it's likely to be calorie-laden. And if you want a cosy restaurant, it probably can't accommodate your office Christmas party.

Be clear about what your core strength is as a brand and then try and identify a related, mirror weakness that amplifies that benefit.

And obviously, you wouldn't want to admit an issue that's fundamental to your offer. So, a bad taste works for medicine, but not for beer. Or, as a budget airline, you could admit to a no-frills service, but you'd never claim to have a poor safety record.

The pratfall effect isn't a bias that you can apply on every campaign. But if you're ever lucky enough to identify a reasonably minor weakness that amplifies your strength then you can harness one of the most powerful tactics in advertising.

THREE KEY TAKEAWAYS

1. **Turn a weakness into a strength**: As the pratfall effect shows, admitting a flaw can boost appeal. Don't shy away from this approach in your creativity. Just make sure your brand has the requisite status to pull off this trick.

2. **Build trust through honesty**: Being upfront about a weakness can build credibility and, consequently, trust. Most ad claims are treated skeptically. You need to close the trust gap and one way to do that is to admit a meaningful weakness. That acts as a proof point for your honesty and then all your other claims are more likely to be believed.

3. **Make sure to pick the right flaw**: Be sure that the flaw you highlight has a positive mirror image. For example, we assume a costly item will be high quality. So, work out what your core strength is and then identify whether there is a corresponding weakness that amplifies that strength.

10

LIQUID DEATH

WATER IS THE stuff of life. So why would you ever reach for a brand called "Liquid Death" to quench your thirst?

Plenty of reasons, as it turns out.

A piece of the fun

In 2009, the *Vans Warped Tour* was in its 15th year. A mix of punk rock and extreme sports fans gathered in Denver, Colorado, to sweat together. Among the heaving crowd was Mike Cessario, then a 26-year-old graphic designer.

With an eye for a logo, he noticed that bands were swigging from Monster cans up on stage — not surprising, as the energy drink brand was a major sponsor. But after a bit of backstage chat, he discovered that, rather than over-caffeinating themselves, performers had filled their Monster cans with water. They were looking for hydration, but none of the water brands of the time fitted the vibe.

And that's when the realization came to Cessario: it was the "unhealthy" brands that had all the marketing fun. Why not water?

In 2014, he was working on a health campaign warning against high-sugar energy drinks. He floated his water idea, suggesting the launch of a brand with all the offbeat, humorous marketing tactics used in the energy drink category. His client, sadly for them, didn't go for it.

But Cessario was confident in his concept. So, over the next few years, he worked on designs in his free time, and by 2017 he had a new brand to trademark.

He still didn't have an actual product, but decided to create an ad that would get people talking. With a budget of $1,500[38] and a mockup of a Liquid Death can, he shot an ad that captured the brand's unique irreverence: "Don't fall for the marketing bullsh*t, water is not yoga."

It worked. Boosted by a social media campaign, after just a few months the ad had three million views.[39] People were begging to buy the product. This amazing response was enough to secure funding to get the idea off the ground for real.

True to its brand essence, Liquid Death launched in bars, tattoo parlors, and liquor stores before rolling out in more mainstream venues. It has been a tearaway success ever since. In 2019, it generated sales of $2.8 million.[40] By 2024, it had broken the $250 million barrier and the company was valued at over $1.4 billion.[41] Cessario claims it's one of the fastest-growing non-alcoholic drinks ever.

The dumbest name

It is immediately apparent that the Liquid Death brand is completely unlike any other water brand. And this is the first key to its success.

The death punk branding — melting skulls, gothic font — the strapline "Murder your thirst" and marketing based on all things irreverent and morbid are at odds with every other water brand out there. The norm is to highlight the health-giving benefits of water: clarity, purity, and the freshness of mountain springs.

But as Cessario puts it: "Why does health food always have to be so quiet and responsible? How come all of this sh*t that's terrible for you is allowed to have all the fun and explosions?"

That's why he came up with what he calls the dumbest name ever for a safe, healthy drink of water: Liquid Death. With packaging you can't ignore and a campaign of comedy stunts that rival the best of MTV's *Jackass*.

In one of these ads, *Jackass* presenter Steve-O himself gets a Liquid Death water tattoo: "All the pain of a regular tattoo, none of the permanence." Another features a "collectable enema kit." Or you can watch Martha Stewart apparently severing the hands of her loyal fans to make Halloween candles (which were sold as merch).

Stick out

So, what's the psychology of its success? In defying convention, Liquid Death has tapped into a powerful behavioral bias: the fact that we recall what is distinctive. The phenomenon is known as the *Von Restorff effect*, after the German psychologist who first found evidence of it back in 1933.

For this original study, participants heard a list of nine related items — for example, animals — and one odd-one-out — say, an item of clothing. They reliably recalled the clothes. And when this was reversed so the odd-one-out was an animal among a list of wardrobe items, it was the animal they remembered.

Even though the original study is 90 years old, the results hold true today. In fact, we've done our own experiments to confirm its relevance. In one, Richard and his colleague Laura Weston gave 500 participants a list of logos: 11 car brands and one fast-food brand. After a pause, they were asked which brands they could recall. They were four times more likely to mention the fast-food brand than the average car brand.

There's also in-market evidence that shows distinctiveness helps ads stick. Research company Zappi analyzed 2,300 US ads and found that those deemed to stand out were more likely to be effective. Across the whole database, the average rating for distinctiveness was 3.81 on a five-point scale (with higher numbers representing greater distinctiveness). However, scores changed when Zappi split the data according to effectiveness. The top 10% of ads had a distinctiveness rating of 4.03 and for the top 1%, it was 4.15. In contrast, the least effective ads — the bottom 5% — had a distinctiveness rating of 3.6.

> Distinctiveness isn't just a nice-to-have. It's a crucial ingredient.

Distinctiveness isn't just a nice-to-have. It's a crucial ingredient for successful communications.

It's easy to see how the distinctiveness advantage works for Liquid Death in the aisles: a row of clear plastic bottles featuring mountain ranges and pastel coloring; and in the middle of them, gold-rimmed cans emblazoned with gothic, black lettering and melting skulls.

Spotting these cans, you might at first think some beers had accidentally been placed among the water bottles. But that's the beauty of it. You'll notice it, and you might well pick it up to take a closer look.

And that is a very deliberate — and highly successful — Liquid Death tactic. As Cessario puts it: "Once someone picks something up, you've basically won." Once a product is in your hand, you automatically consider it as an option. Noticeability really matters.

Simply encouraging consideration — even if all the attention isn't 100% positive — is a strategy that has worked across other media too, including their Super Bowl advertising. Andy Pearson, Liquid Death's creative director, told us:

> When we did the Super Bowl, we had angry people tweeting 'Who would dare sell water back to us?' Which is a win, because it means people are reconsidering the product. That was the point — to get people to make more critical choices. It made people rethink the entire category.

A certain confidence

Another bias is at play here. Consider the sheer chutzpah of branding your water to look like a beer — not many would have the nerve.

But maybe they should. Because there's evidence that standing out from the crowd, as well as getting you noticed, will garner respect from your customers. And that's because of a bias known as the *red sneakers effect*.

This suggests that nonconformity can signal status. The theory is that only those with enough clout can afford to challenge convention — and get away with it. They have sufficient respect in the bank to take that risk. Think about a work setting. If the intern flouts the dress code, they get sent home. But what if the CEO does it? The likelihood is, they'll get away with it.

To test the red sneakers effect in a commercial setting, Richard ran a study in 2020 with Duncan Willett and Sumran Kaul from News UK.

They showed participants four bottles of craft beer with colorful designs. Three of the labels were designed in broadly the same style (style A), whereas the final beer had a markedly different style (style *B*). So, let's call this selection of designs A A A *B*. Bottle *B* stands out. Participants then had to rate the quality of the four beers.

Figure 4: An illustration of the first test AAA*B*. Bottle *B* breaks convention

Source: Adapted from Shotton, Willett and Kaul (2020).

In a second setup, another group of participants were shown four beer bottles. This time, two of the beers from the first experiment were included: the uniquely styled bottle (style *B*) and one of the others (style A). The remaining two beers looked similar in style to *B*. So, this selection was *B* A *B* *B* — so bottle *B* blends in (and A stands out).

Figure 5: An illustration of the second test *B*ABB. Bottle *B* conforms to the convention

*Bottle B: The same bottle B as test 1.

Source: Adapted from Shotton, Willett and Kaul (2020).

This experimental design allowed for the ratings of the same bottle design (***B***) to be compared when it was either breaking convention (the first scenario) or conforming (the second scenario).

Just as the red sneakers effect would predict, bottle design ***B*** was rated higher in the first scenario, when it broke the surrounding convention.

In this experiment, nonconformity conferred a 5% improvement in perceived quality. This was a small effect, but the convention broken was minor; the comparison was with three other bottles in the test. It wasn't a wide-scale societal flouting of convention. Maybe a bigger break from the norm can reap bigger benefits.

And Liquid Death has achieved this. The brand has built a powerfully effective personality based largely — but, importantly, not solely — on non-conformity. Its flouting of category conventions makes it stand out, and adds to its cool.

But this distinctiveness is not something the brand has done in isolation; it's a key ingredient, but not the whole marketing cake.

Love what you know

So, we've seen that smashing conventional boundaries can lead you toward success. But how best should you go about this?

Well, you need to give customers the confidence to judge your nonconformity as deliberate rather than an ill-informed error. And this is where consistency becomes important. If the Liquid Death packaging was randomly different, but the rest of the marketing was business-as-usual, snowy-mountain-top branding, we wouldn't be convinced.

Liquid Death doesn't just break conventions — it does so consistently. Essentially, the brand has taken the persona of an irreverent beer and applied it to a new category: water.

This provides a framework for building the brand. It's the adoption of another category's norms that helps Liquid Death to maintain absolute consistency — and, with it, the opportunity to repeat the message often, and in a structured way.

The team maintains such consistency, creative director Andy Pearson told us, by imagining Liquid Death as a character:

> To find new ways to express the brand, we think, 'what would Liquid Death do?' There's almost always a correct answer. So, it becomes an easy process — we don't have to think about the strategy because we know what this character would do. It's unlocked so much stuff.

This consistent approach allows the brand to leverage another bias, and one that is relevant for every advertiser: the *mere exposure effect*. Whether you like the creative approach that Liquid Death has chosen or not, evidence shows that humans have a tendency to develop a preference for things simply by becoming familiar with them. This means the more that Liquid Death exposes us to consistent messaging, the more likable it will be.

The original study was conducted by University of Michigan psychologist Robert Zajonc in 1968. He showed participants pictures of faces, and asked them to rate how pleasant they were. However, some of the participants had seen the faces before and some had not. Among those who had seen the images before, some had seen them a few times, some as many as 25 times.

The findings of Zajonc's studies were clear: the greater the previous exposure, the more positive the response. Zajonc re-ran this study in two other settings, showing participants nonsense words and Chinese characters. Each time he found the same result.

> **People have a tendency to develop a preference for things simply by becoming familiar with them.**

Chart 5: The more we see a stimulus, the warmer we feel towards it

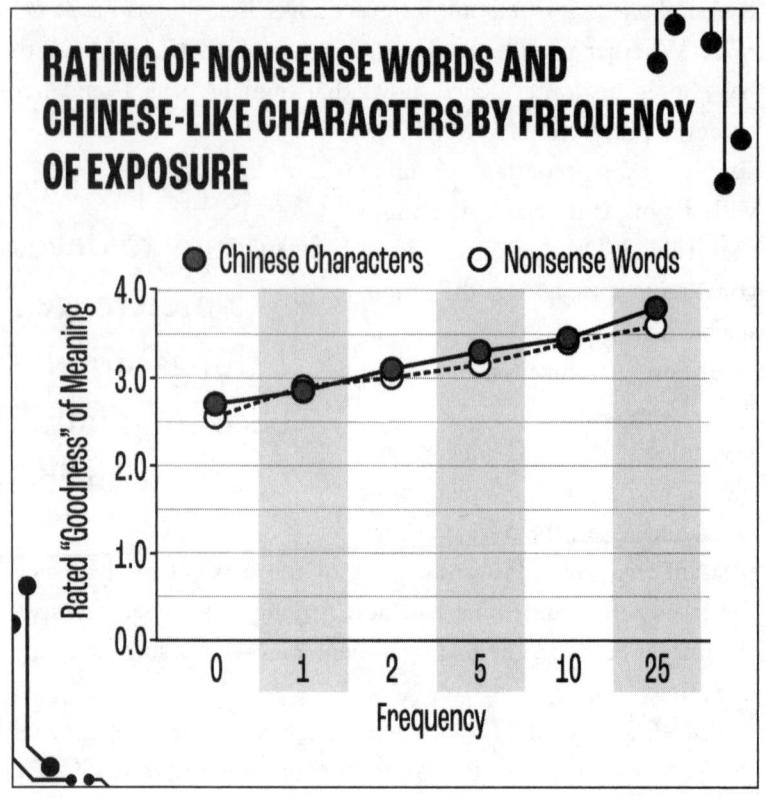

Source: Adapted from Zajonc (1968).

It seems that just seeing something regularly makes us like it more — even if no extra information is imparted. One explanation for this is that the more we're exposed to a stimulus, the more easily we process it. And that ease is interpreted as liking.

This is fundamental to the effectiveness of advertising and one of the key arguments for marketing consistency.

It's an approach wholeheartedly adopted in Liquid Death's marketing strategy. The brand's distinctiveness is effective because it's not haphazard; it's intentional, consistent, and persistent.

So, one of the main lessons from Liquid Death is for brands to stick with a creative idea for longer.

Brands have a tendency to chop and change their messaging approach too much. Perhaps that's because of the personality types who are attracted to work in the field, many of whom have a disproportionate love of novelty. Or maybe it's because marketers tire of their approach quickly because they think about their brand 24/7, whereas shoppers rarely give most products a second thought.

Whatever the reason, marketers need to recognise that there's a downside to changing their campaign. The same creative idea will become more appealing as it becomes familiar, so when you change your approach, you may lose goodwill.

Why don't brands break convention more often?

The case for not conforming to category norms seems convincing. So why don't more brands take the plunge?

To conforming brands, it may feel like a risk to swim against the tide. But as Pearson puts it:

> The riskiest thing to do is not take a risk. The only way to do it is to take a counterintuitive, contrarian viewpoint. People say we're insane to put water in cans. I think we'd be insane not to.

Most brands have an instinctive fear of doing something different, as there's a strong natural drive to copy what the majority do. This urge to conform is called social proof — because we look to others for evidence that our behavior is acceptable — and it's a powerful drive to overcome as a brand. If you want to read more about the phenomenon, we cover it in Chapter 6 on Aperol. In that chapter, we discuss the effect of social proof among consumers. However, it's just as influential among professionals.

Evidence comes from a study run by the Australian government, which sought to reduce antibiotic-prescribing behavior among doctors. In 2018 it sent out thousands of letters to general practitioners. Some doctors received a letter outlining the dangers of antibiotic overprescription. Among this group, there was a 3.2% reduction in prescription rates compared to the control.

However, other doctors received a letter that also harnessed social proof: they were told they were prescribing more antibiotics than their peers. This was far more successful, producing a 9.3% reduction in prescription rates.

Chart 6: Even professionals are affected by social proof

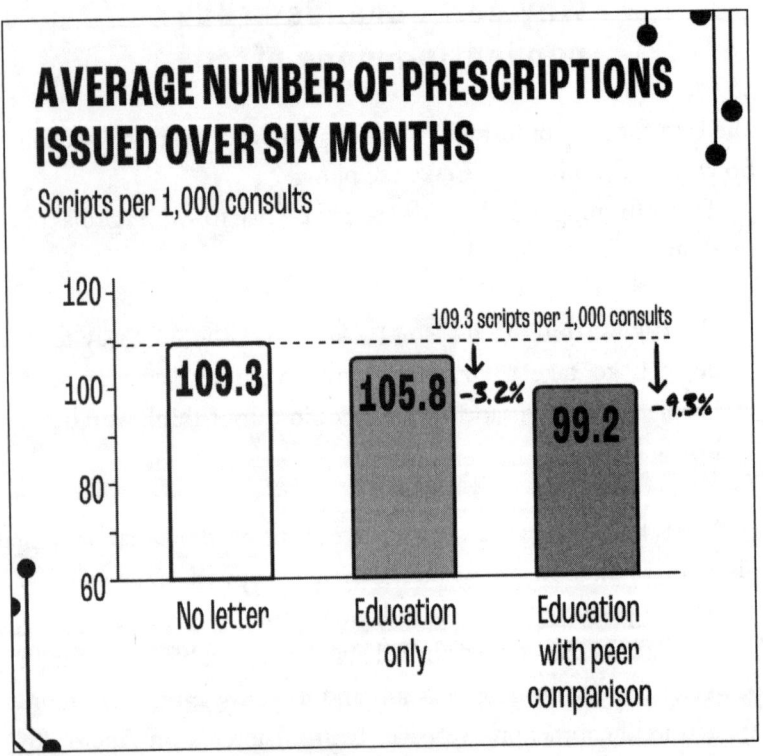

Source: Adapted from Australian Government (2018).

The results show how professionals are influenced by their peers. And if even doctors — who pride themselves on evidence-based decisions — are affected by the crowd, you can be sure that marketers are too.

The power of this driver is one of the reasons why it's so hard to go out on a limb and shun the tried-and-tested approach of our brand's category.

But there's another reason why ads in a category start to look the same. It's what Jim Carroll, ex-chairman of ad agency BBH, calls the *wind tunnel effect*. He's referring to an observation from the 1980s, when cars started to change shape — and all began to look alike. Because they'd all been tested in the same wind tunnel and every designer was shaping the body to improve the same outcome: aerodynamics.

As with car design, the field of marketing has developed certain practices for testing ads to check if consumers like them. By asking people directly if they'd be motivated to buy, advertisers are gearing their work toward what consumers say they want.

But that's not the same as what actually motivates them to buy. We all know that we humans are terrible at predicting our own future behavior. So, why do we continue to use direct questioning to guide us? The approach results in ads that become increasingly interchangeable. We lose the power of differentiation.

So, stop asking people what they want and instead run simple test-and-control experiments. There are some smart ways to do this, which all brands should work into their design development. But let's not discuss that here — more of that in the next chapter...

THREE KEY TAKEAWAYS

1. **Be distinctive**: The argument from the Von Restorff effect is that we are hardwired to notice what is distinctive. If you want to be noticed, identify your category conventions and then decide which you can break.

2. **Be consistent**: It's not enough to be distinctive in a haphazard way. Instead, you need to behave consistently. This will help you tap into the mere exposure effect, which shows that we exhibit a preference for things we have seen frequently.

3. **Don't follow the crowd**: Watch out for our tendency to conform. How can you create a culture at your company where people feel comfortable to deviate from the herd?

11

DYSON

When the Dyson DC01 vacuum launched in the UK in 1994, it put people in a spin. Folks seemed to find it satisfying to watch the machinery whirring and see the dirt sucked up inside.

For the final design, James Dyson had decided to keep the cylinder transparent, despite advice against it at the time — but it seems he knew a thing or two about consumer psychology. Maybe that's why his fortunes have grown to an estimated $15 billion.[42]

What did he know that his advisors didn't?

Developing a cyclone

As a student, Dyson was obviously diligent with his housework. Because he noticed something. Over time, his vacuum cleaner — a Hoover — would lose suction and become less and less effective. Keen to get to the bottom of this, he removed the vacuum bag to take a look. The bag was blocked with dust, reducing the machine's capacity to draw air through it. Dyson filed it away as a problem to be solved.

Some years later, he visited a sawmill, where he observed a giant cyclone being used to extract sawdust from the air. He wondered if the same approach could be miniaturized and put to work cleaning floors. So, he tested the idea at home with a cardboard prototype attached to his standard vacuum. It worked.

Convinced now that this new approach could help him reimagine the vacuum cleaner, Dyson began designing, testing, and redesigning. And testing. And redesigning. Picking up funding along the way, he continued the iteration process... 15 years, and 5,127 prototypes later, the first bagless vacuum cleaner was launched: the Dyson DC01.

You can see from the thousands of times he tried and failed to fix the vacuum problem that Dyson has always been open to embracing failure. He once said: "Developing an idea and making it work takes time and patience... And we fail every day. Failure is the best medicine — as long as you learn something."[43]

Dyson's personal prototyping ethos is embedded in the company today. He explained: "We develop technology iteratively — making the smallest changes, building prototype after prototype until we have got it as close to perfect as we can muster."

It's this iterative approach, accepting failures as necessary steps along the way, that ultimately results in success. The company has a reputation for putting painstaking effort into every product, to get it just right. But this is similar for Dyson's competitors too. So, what sets the brand apart?

One key difference is the fact that customers know about this meticulous approach, and appreciate it.

A clear win

Dyson actively chose to be transparent about the way he worked: the marketing for the DC01 highlighted the huge number of redesigns

CHAPTER 11: DYSON

it took to develop the cleaner. Not only does Dyson mention the 5,127 prototypes in the very first line of his autobiography, but repeated testing is central to the way the brand talks about its products. There's a whole section on the Dyson website dedicated to what it calls "relentless engineering."

The idea was even the focus of one of the company's most important ads. The copy read:

> While other vacuum manufacturers toyed with things like height adapters or new attachments, James Dyson worked on solving the real problem with vacuums — they lose suction power. After testing over 5,000 prototypes, he created the first vacuum cleaner that doesn't lose suction. And now, it's here in America. So, come see a Dyson today. It's the vacuum. Reinvented.

What's going on?

Maybe it matters more when your design is novel. Making it clear that the product has been through more than 5,000 prototypes before landing on its latest iteration should help allay any sense that this is a harebrained, mad-scientist project that could blow up in your kitchen.

But as well as offering reassurance, there's another important reason to highlight work done: effort equates to value in customers' minds. This is due to a bias called the *illusion of effort*.

One study providing evidence of its impact was conducted by Justin Kruger and colleagues at the University of Illinois Urbana-Champaign in 2004.

The team recruited 138 participants and split them into two groups. Both groups were given a poem to read called "Order" by

Effort equates to value in customers' minds.

Michael Van Walleghen. One group was told it took the poet four hours to write; the second group was told it took 18 hours.

Next, participants rated the poem on a scale from 1 to 11 (1 = hate it; 11 = love it).

Additionally, they were asked to estimate how much money the poem would earn if sold to a poetry magazine.

The results revealed that people who thought the poem took four hours to compose (low effort group) gave an average rating of 5.84. However, those told that it took 18 hours (high effort group) scored it at 6.43 — an uplift of 10%.

In addition, the low effort group estimated the poem would make $50 if sold to a magazine, while the high effort group thought it was worth $95 — a 90% increase in value.

Table 12: Effort is used as a proxy for quality

	LOW EFFORT	HIGH EFFORT
Quality rating	5.84 →	6.43 +10%
Perceived value	$50 →	$95 +90%

Source: Adapted from Kruger (2004).

The key point is: the exact same piece of work was rated better and valued more highly when people were told that more effort had gone into it. But Kruger explores impressions of a poem — a somewhat esoteric focus. You might sensibly wonder if this can be extrapolated to commercial settings.

We wondered the same and carried out our own experiment to explore the issue. For our study, we showed 278 Americans a picture of a fictitious brand, Black Sheep Vodka. Half of the group were told the brand had tested 143 designs before choosing (high effort);

the other half were not (low effort). We then asked how much they liked the bottle design.

Figure 6: Bottle design of Black Sheep Vodka

Source: Barnes (2015).

Among the low-effort group, 17% liked or loved it. That figure climbed to 23% for the high-effort group — that's a 35% improvement.

The higher rating occurs because it's difficult to judge the quality of the design. And, as Daniel Kahneman says, "When faced with a difficult question, we often answer an easier one instead, usually without noticing the substitution." In this case, the easier question is how much effort did the designer expend. We use effort as a proxy for quality. The same substitution happens in many commercial settings.

The key for any brand, then, is to be transparent about the lengths you've gone to in creating your product. It's not enough to expend lots of effort; you have to let your customer know.

But what if apparently little effort goes into your product? Say, if you're a fast-food outlet that serves your customers in seconds? Itsu, an Asian-inspired lunchtime takeaway chain, is a great example. Your miso soup or rice bowl is served instantly, so it's hard to claim that chefs have toiled over it for hours. But Itsu has come up with a great way to work around the problem, still applying the illusion of effort. It focuses on the hours that go into becoming the kind of miso master who works for Itsu. Sandwich boards standing outside stores say:

744,600 hours.

Apparently, it takes 10,000 hours to master a skill.

Our miso master Yoshihiro would disagree. He and his family have been making miso in Japan for 85 years (744,600 hours) and they're still getting better.

You might want to consider the same approach when it comes to negotiating with clients. Consider the story of designer Paula Scher and the $1.5 million napkin.[44] Scher's company, Pentagram, had been briefed to come up with a brand design for the newly formed Citibank. Over a lunch meeting with the client, she supposedly sketched a quick logo on a paper napkin. Her speedy design turned into the basis of the entire brand. The client may have been less than delighted — $1.5 million seemed a lot for such a quick turnaround.

CHAPTER 11: DYSON

But, Paula is famously quoted as saying, "It took me a few seconds to draw it, but it took me 34 years to learn how to do that in a few seconds." Thankfully, Citibank understood this, and the logo has since become one of the most recognizable in finance.

This story reminds us that if we provide services speedily, we need to draw attention to the time that has been spent elsewhere to reach this level of efficiency. Otherwise, there's a risk that the quality of work is underappreciated.

It's also something to keep in mind when using AI. The speed and efficiency inherent in AI can sometimes mean it falls foul of the illusion of effort. That might feel like a leap. But there's a study from Kobe Millet and colleagues at Vrije Universiteit Amsterdam that suggest just that.

In 2023, the researchers recruited 800 participants online and showed them two almost identical drawings of a human skull, both created by human artists. However, one of the images was randomly labelled as AI-generated and one as human-created.

> The speed and efficiency inherent in AI can sometimes mean it falls foul of the illusion of effort.

Participants rated their appreciation of the creativity of each piece of art, as well as purchase intent, on scales from one to seven.

For creativity, artworks labeled as hand-drawn were rated at 5.30, whereas those labeled as AI-generated scored 2.75 — that's a massive 48% drop. And, most worryingly, researchers saw the same pattern for purchase intent. The images marked as hand-drawn received a score of 4.85. Those marked as AI-generated scored 3.02. People would be 38% less likely to pay for them.

Table 13: AI creations suffer because they're assumed to have been low effort

	LABELED AS HAND-DRAWN	LABELED AS AI-GENERATED
Creativity	5.30 →	2.75 -48%
Purchase intent	4.85 →	3.02 -38%

Source: Adapted from Millet (2023).

People assume that AI output is low effort. After all, they know that ChatGPT can write a blog post in seconds. This means people don't value AI outputs as highly as human efforts.

If you're going to be open with your clients, or the public, about using AI tools, it's important to emphasize the work you've put in before getting to the output, or in monitoring its results. For example, how many years of experience do you need to develop successful prompts? What expertise do you need to assess the suitability of AI results?

Transparency in everything

So far, we've talked about consumers needing to *understand* the effort that goes into something. But what about actually *seeing* the work as it goes on?

Dyson always intended to make behind-the-scenes design work as visible as possible. He did this in two ways.

Not only did he advertise the amount of work that had gone into the DC01, he also designed it with a clear dust collection cylinder. Some of the team were uncomfortable with this feature. After all, they argued, who wants to look at the nasty stuff you're sucking up off the floor? But Dyson held on to the idea and his product became an iconic piece of design.

Dyson's see-through cylinder is a beautiful example of the impact of showcasing work, and is arguably the single most important success factor of the original vacuum. He was always keen to show the machine's inner workings and is proud of the technology on display. It's something he also admires in the work of others — he once said: "Brunel's bridges look so inspiring because you can see the maths and science behind them. Every arc, nut, bolt, and girder tells a story. Design should not be afraid to bare its innards."

There are other fields in which working processes are showcased. A good example is in dining, where some restaurants have an open kitchen allowing customers to witness the chefs in action.

Is this something more brands should try to capitalize on? Evidence suggests so. A 2015 study by Ryan Buell and Tami Kim at Harvard Business School explored operational transparency in a real-world setting.

In a cafeteria, the researchers asked 299 diners how satisfied they were with their food on a scale from one to seven (one = very dissatisfied; seven = very satisfied). Sometimes respondents could see their food being prepared (and the kitchen staff could see the diners); other times, they couldn't see each other.

When customers couldn't see what was going on, they gave an average rating of 4.57. But when diners could watch the chefs in action, they rated their satisfaction as 5.49 — 20% higher than when food prep was behind the scenes.

But of course, this kind of transparency is not feasible for many products and services. Thankfully, there's evidence that an alternative approach might be almost as effective.

Ryan Buell and Michael Norton explored the illusion of effort in a 2011 study. They recruited 266 participants and asked them to book a holiday using a simulated travel comparison site. Participants waited between 0 and 60 seconds for results and, during the delay, were shown either a simple, uninformative progress bar or a continually changing list of the sites being searched (the transparency version). Finally, the participants rated the value of the service they received on a scale from one to seven (one = very low value; seven = very high value).

Those who saw only the progress bar gave an average rating of 4.96. However, those who saw the progress bar and the constantly changing search list (transparency version) rated the site as 5.36. This represents an 8% uplift compared to the blind version.

So, showing a process as it happens affects how highly people value a service. And there are plenty of creative ways to apply this, including user experience (UX) solutions like the one in Buell and Norton's study. It's worth considering transparency at the design stage of any product or service.

Getting to the truth

There's another area in which Dyson has applied some sound findings from behavioral science: research. He is skeptical of market research, saying in one interview: "We do a little bit of research, but are careful not to be led by it. Most focus groups are wrong. You just can't ask people what they want and then go off and make it."[45] And in another interview: "You have to be careful with market research… Merely giving people what they want isn't always enough." Dyson would rather rely on the expertise of his designers, as well as plenty of trial and error through repeated prototyping. After all, he argues, customers and focus groups didn't ask for a bagless vacuum cleaner because they hadn't imagined it possible.

There is a warning here for all marketers: when it comes to market research, we cannot fully trust what people say.

One of the broad themes in behavioral science is that what people say motivates them and what *actually* motivates them can be two different things. If you look at most of the studies in this book, researchers don't tend to ask. Instead, they set up two different scenarios and monitor how a group of people respond in each.

You can do the same in your research by using monadic testing. This involves randomly splitting participants into groups, with each group seeing one version of what you are testing — the other groups see a different version. The only difference between the two versions should be the one factor you are exploring — for example, a particular image, choice of wording, or position of an item on a page.

You can then observe how respondents behave, or ask them to give ratings. Any difference between the groups can then be attributed to the changed variable.

An example of monadic testing can be found in the research described on the illusion of effort for our made-up brand, Black Sheep Vodka. All participants saw the same ad. The only difference was that half were told the design had been through 143 iterations (high effort); the other half were not (low effort). The high effort group preferred the design.

If we'd shown participants both setups side-by-side, they probably would not have liked one more than the other, because the images are the same — the impact of the multiple design iterations, even if participants knew about them, would have been lost.

It's important to observe behavior in as natural a setting as possible rather than asking customers to rationalize their preference — not because participants lie, but simply because no one has a full understanding of the subconscious biases that influence their decisions and opinions.

THREE KEY TAKEAWAYS

1. **Tell people about your efforts**: The more time and expertise that appear to have gone into creating your product or service, the more your customers will value it, so tell customers about your efforts.

2. **Pull back the curtain**: Don't just tell customers about your efforts, show them. Think about how you can adapt your design or UX to showcase your work.

3. **Watch what people do, not what they say**: When conducting research, set up tests to observe what customers actually do — don't just ask them.

12

FACEBOOK

Have you shared any family news on Facebook recently? Perhaps a few holiday pics? Even if you haven't, there's a good chance you'll have seen someone else's. Because almost half the population on the planet uses it.

There are many complex factors behind Facebook's stratospheric rise. But a few key biases helped it on the way and keep us coming back again and again.

Early networks

Connecting people has always been Mark Zuckerberg's thing. He started young, helping out at his father's home-based dental business: writing code to allow household members to use the home computer to speak to the office one. It was essentially an early instant messenger, which the family named ZuckNet.

Interestingly, Zuckerberg majored in psychology at Harvard, keeping computer science courses going alongside. It was while studying here that he developed the notorious FaceMash program that got him into hot water with the college. He described this as a "prank website" — it included pictures of students and invited users to rate their attractiveness. Zuckerberg took it down pretty fast, but not before it had come to the attention of the Administrative Board.[46]

Lucky for Zuck, he was allowed to stay on at school and he began to develop early versions of what would become Facebook. The idea was to create a digital resource listing student details, designed to replace the paper-based directory at Harvard called The Facebook.

He launched thefacebook.com first to the students in his house, and from there it grew fast. Within 24 hours, there were almost 1,500 sign-ups.[47] Initially, the service was limited to Harvard, but it quickly expanded to include other colleges, and in 2005 facebook.com went live to the public.

By December 2005, there were reportedly six million active users.[48] Today, there are over three billion.[49]

Valuable connections

While the website had started simply as a place to find other students in the same classes or clubs, it quickly became much more than that.

Facebook allowed people to post photos and share information about themselves on their "Wall," and it soon introduced the ability for people to "tag" themselves and their friends, making these images searchable by other users.

The platform took off as usership grew and marketers jumped on board, realizing they could communicate directly with interested customers on a scale that had never been possible before.

But a real gamechanger emerged in 2009, when developers added the "Like" button. This feature, which lets users publicly signal their approval, hadn't appeared on any platform previously.

It's an easy way to show appreciation without having to comment. Of course, Likes fast became a measure of popularity and are now a fundamental feature of social media.

By May 2012, Facebook was valued at $104 billion.[50] It hardly seems possible, but usership has continued to grow since and as of 2025, its market capitalization stands at $1.28 trillion.[51]

Show the love

People really do love Facebook. In a 2018 study, Jay Corrigan and colleagues at Kenyon College ran a study to find out how much users would need to be paid to give up the platform for a year.

They asked 931 participants to take part in a real online auction, where they bid on how much they would need to step away from their Facebook account for a full year. Researchers then watched the winner deactivate their account and could check throughout the year that they hadn't reactivated it.

A notable number of participants — 145 — were not willing to bid at all, so attached were they to their accounts. Among the remaining recruits, the average bid was $1,921. That's a hefty price tag.

Our ongoing love of Facebook explains why Zuckerberg's net worth is estimated to be close to $200 billion.[52] But how has Facebook become so embedded in people's lives that they can't manage without it? Why is it so irresistible? Let's look at a few biases that help answer this question.

Reaping rewards from uncertainty

Yes, we like to look at Facebook to catch up on news from friends and family, and to follow interest groups and brands. But the real draw happens when we post. That's because our dopamine system kicks in when we're in a state of excited anticipation. And every time we post something on social media, this is the state we're in, to some extent. How many Likes or other reactions will we get?

The addictive nature of Facebook may in part be down to the powerful drive of *uncertain rewards* — that is, we are more motivated to behave in a particular way when we're not sure what the reward will be.

One early study demonstrating that this is hardwired in animals was conducted by Michael Zeiler in 1972. Working at Emory University at the time, he set out to explore the best way to motivate behavior and decided to conduct an experiment using three lab-raised pigeons. In his experiment, the pigeons could win a tasty pellet of food when they pecked a button. Zeiler started with the obvious approach: a reward every time they pecked. This he called the 100% group. He tracked how often they pecked when they knew they would always get fed.

Then, he changed things up. Instead of giving food every time, Zeiler set the button to deliver pellets randomly. Sometimes the birds would peck and get nothing; other times they would be rewarded. The frequency varied: pigeons would be randomly rewarded 90%, 70%, 50%, 30%, or 10% of the time. Once again, he monitored how many times they hit the button.

The results were fascinating — and somewhat surprising. Reducing the reward frequency from 100% down to 90%, 70%, or 50% *increased* the pigeons' responses. On average, the birds pecked nearly twice as much when the reward was unpredictable. It seemed that the animals got hooked on the uncertainty.

However, the increase in responses was true only up to a point. When the reward frequency dropped to 30% or 10%, the birds started to lose interest and pecked less, disengaged by the lack of reinforcement.

All well and good for pigeons — what about people? Well, a similar phenomenon is seen in humans, and there's plenty of evidence of this too. In 2017, Nina Mazar from the University of Toronto and colleagues conducted a study on the influence of uncertain rewards in the real world.

The researchers placed a vending machine in a student lounge. The machine featured ten options, with two buttons allocated for each candy. The treats cost 75 cents each.

Then, during a two-week period, the researchers introduced a sales promotion. Customers were given a choice between paying a lower price of 50 cents per candy (fixed reward) or the regular price of 75 cents, but with a one-in-three chance of receiving the item for free (uncertain reward).

> **If there's a chance of something great, we'll take that over the certainty of something just good.**

The researchers observed how many times people went for each option.

Although the two promotional offers were of mathematically equivalent value, customers preferred the chance to win a free treat over a definite reduction in price. Results showed that 84 candies were sold under the fixed discount option versus 120 with the uncertain reward option — that's 43% more.

It's not necessarily logical, but we are drawn to the excitement of a gamble. If there's a chance of something *great*, we'll take that over the certainty of something just *good*.

This in part explains what draws us back to Facebook time and again. When we share something, we know people will see our post. But we don't know what the response might be — we don't know how many Likes, hearts or laughs we'll get. There's a chance it could be a fantastic, life-affirming confidence boost for us, so we just have to keep checking.

But, as we saw with the pigeons, too little reward can be

demotivating. If your post generated no reactions at all, you would probably hesitate before sharing next time.

It's worth keeping this in mind when offering rewards or discounts on your brand, as the principle applies to any area, not just small vending machine items. In the same paper by Mazar, researchers tested uncertain versus fixed promotions with pens costing $10 and DVD rentals at $4.50 and found a similar preference for uncertain rewards.

Given the strength of the evidence, it's surprising how few brands operate this kind of promotion mechanic. The cost to a business of offering 10% off everything is exactly the same as offering one in ten customers the contents of their basket for free. The latter will be far more enticing to customers and is likely to generate more sales. Perhaps the fact that it just "feels bigger" to financial decision-makers should be seen as the very reason to go ahead.

Or, what about offering a gambling or lottery-style discount? During the 2007 Super Bowl and World Series, some retailers in New England offered a full refund to a lucky few customers in the event that either the Patriots or the Red Sox won. This proved highly effective for the businesses. For example, Jordan's Furniture took 30,000 orders[53] during the six-week promotion period and one customer, who took the opportunity to furnish his entire house, ended up with a $40,000 refund when the Red Sox triumphed.[54]

If you don't want to rely on national events, you could copy what one UK restaurant has done and introduce your own little gambling-style game. Dishoom is a chain of Indian restaurants that has applied the power of uncertain rewards with a bit of creative flair. Get your hands on one of its "secret" keyrings — which you only need to ask for — and the next time you visit, you can show it when asking for the check. You'll get the chance to roll a dice — a six wins the whole table's bill for free, drinks and all. Diners keep going back to try their luck, whether they win or not.

CHAPTER 12: FACEBOOK

Regret nothing

Another way to set up effective promotions is to use what's known as a *regret lottery* — an especially powerful way to employ a gambling-style tactic.

In a regret lottery, everyone is entered and a winner randomly selected, but they only get the prize if they meet the criteria (say, making a purchase). If they haven't, the person is told what they *would* have won — but missed out on.

Regret lotteries harness the strong motivation of *loss aversion*. This describes the fact that we fear losses more than we value an equal gain. And because of this, the anticipation of a loss strongly impacts behavior.

Exploring this, psychologist Uri Gneezy of the University of California, San Diego, conducted a study with a large company that runs daily training workshops. The aim was to reduce car usage via a regret lottery.

Over one week, workshop attendees were asked to avoid using their car to reduce traffic and pollution. Gneezy then split the participants into four groups:

1. Control: No incentive given.
2. $5 fixed reward: Participants were given $5 every day that they did not drive into work.
3. $500 lottery: For every day that participants didn't drive into work, they would receive an entry into the $500 lottery.
4. $500 regret lottery: Every participant was entered in the lottery. But when the lottery was drawn, only someone who had not driven into work was eligible to win the $500.

All incentive groups performed better than the control. The $5 a day group used parking 10% less than the control and the $500 lottery reduced parking by 18%. However, the $500 regret lottery performed the best by far, reducing parking by 26% compared to the control.

The reason the regret lottery works better than a standard lottery is because, in the latter, you never find out if you would have won. With a regret lottery, you're automatically entered but you can't get the prize if you haven't adopted the behavior. But you do know what you could have won. So, you regret not having done whatever action was needed to be eligible. You didn't just miss a reward. You lost it.

A great example of this principle in action is the Dutch Postcode Lottery. For this regular prize draw, whole streets are automatically picked as winners. But you can only claim the winnings if you've entered. If not, you'll find out what your neighbors have won — but not you. Pretty hard to swallow.

In fact, there's evidence to show just how hard. In a 2004 survey, Marcel Zeelenberg at Tilburg University asked 200 people how much they would regret not entering the Postcode Lottery (a regret lottery) or the State Lottery (a standard lottery). Regret was 55% higher for the Postcode Lottery.

And when asked to imagine their neighbor had won big, participants felt 85% more regret with respect to the Postcode Lottery than the State Lottery — presumably because they know they would have won too, if only they'd entered.

Maybe that explains why over 4.1 million people subscribe to the Dutch lottery,[55] a significant portion of the country's 18-million population. People seem keen to avoid the terrible disappointment of knowing they could have won a life-changing sum, but didn't.

This tactic can be particularly effective when motivating behavior among employees, as seen with the parking example; although it can be harder to influence customers.

There's something else you can try. Because it seems that a near-miss in one area can be generally motivating, even impacting behaviors that are not directly related to the almost-win.

This can be seen in a 2015 study by Monica Wadhwa and JeeHye Christine Kim at the INSEAD Business School in France.

Conducting their study in an accessories shop, they stopped 164 shoppers on their way in and gave them a scratch-off lottery card to play. The shoppers would win $20 if they revealed the same number, six times in a vertical row. The researchers had adjusted each ticket so that it contained a win, a near win, or a clear loss. Figure 7 illustrates examples of the different scratch cards.

Figure 7: Scratch-off lottery cards used in the Wadhwa study

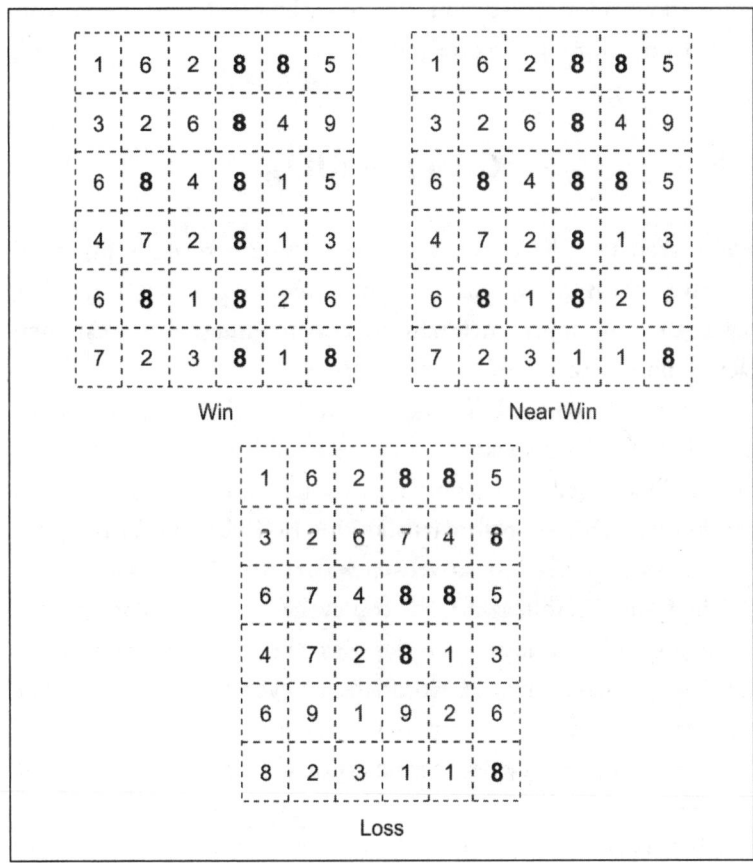

Source: Adapted from Wadhwa (2015).

Next, the researchers observed the shoppers' purchasing behavior. They found that those who had "near-win" cards were likely to spend more in the store than those who had either a "win" or a "loss" card.

The authors speculate that when we get so close to a reward that we can "almost taste it," we get a strong and highly motivational dopamine rush. This is even stronger than when we get the reward. Think of that deal you almost clinched, or the lottery draw you almost won. There's a strong sense of excitement and anticipation, and you're driven to try again.

From a business perspective, this offers evidence that if you are going to use a lottery-style mechanic, dialing up the near wins will keep people coming back for more.*

Keep it rolling

We've seen that Facebook uses the uncertain rewards principle to drive return visits, and we've explored some other ways that businesses can apply uncertain rewards for internal or customer-facing initiatives.

But there's another UX concept that makes Facebook and other digital platforms so sticky: the infinite scroll. The infinite scroll was reportedly devised by designer Aza Raskin and was introduced to Facebook in 2006 — before its adoption by Twitter and Instagram — to replace the need to actively click over to the next page.

The infinite scroll, as it feeds you ever more of the content you crave, arguably harnesses another bias, the very essence of good UX: "make it easy." In other words, design everything to ensure that the least possible effort is required by the user to continue.

There is plenty of evidence from both online and offline behavior

---

* This principle warrants caution. Apply it carefully and make sure you're encouraging people to behave in ways that are in their long-term interest.

to suggest that any amount of friction — such as clicking "Next" to move forward a page — will slow progression. One interesting demonstration of this can be seen in a study led by Andrew Geier at Yale University.

Looking at consumption behavior, the researchers recruited 59 undergraduate students and split them into two groups. The first group was given a regular tube of stacked Lays chips. The second group received the same tube, but with every seventh chip dyed red.

The researchers observed how many chips were consumed in each group. On average, participants in the regular Lays group ate 45 chips per person. But those in the group with every seventh chip dyed consumed an average of only 20 chips — a reduction of around 56%.

When every fifth chip was dyed red, the results were even more significant — people ate just 18 chips, 59% less than the uncolored group.

The study illustrates how even the tiniest amount of friction stops people in their flow and gets them to consider whether continuing is appropriate.

Facebook has applied this "make it easy" principle not only to scrolling, but in hundreds of other ways. Intuitive icons, clear fonts, simple menus — every user interface element has been devised with "make it easy" in mind.

This is something any business can put into action. Think about your entire customer journey. Identify any pain points, however small and insignificant they may seem — because even one extra click will put people off. And remove every bump in the road.

THREE KEY TAKEAWAYS

1. **Keep it unpredictable**: Use uncertain rewards to drive repeat behaviors. The urge to find out how good things might be will drive customers back to you.

2. **Regret motivates action**: Use a regret lottery as a powerful tool to influence behavior. If it's possible — for example, when introducing a change to employees — enter every person into a draw they can win only if they carry out the desired action.

3. **Make it easy**: Smooth even the tiniest wrinkle from the pathway you wish customers to take. Friction tends to have a bigger than expected effect.

13

KLARNA

WHO DOESN'T LOVE the feeling of getting something for nothing? That's what Klarna is banking on — literally.

Undaunted by doubters

While studying at the Stockholm School of Economics, Sebastian Siemiatkowski began to hatch an idea. He took a job at Burger King to help pay his way, and it was while flipping burgers beside fellow student Niklas Adalberth that the pair grew his idea into a plan.

The concept was simple: give e-commerce customers the option to buy online and defer payment until later. They believed that letting shoppers try before they buy would boost trust and benefit the retailer. It aligned with Swedish consumers' reluctance to resort to credit cards, giving an option that wouldn't risk damaging their credit scores.

The pair — together with Victor Jacobsson — believed they had a strong business offer. So in early 2005, Siemiatkowski and his co-founders decided to test their proposition in the annual Stockholm

School of Economics entrepreneurship competition. This *Shark Tank*-style event required a pitch presentation which they delivered to, among others, the king of Sweden. But it didn't go down well.

In fact, they came last. The judges, who were leading Swedish financiers, were not convinced. They reasoned that if the idea was ever going to work, then surely banks would be best placed to do it. There was no need, they argued, for a whole new organization to develop the service. Thankfully, though, there were others who believed in their idea. One enlightened audience member apparently observed: "The banks will never do it!" Presumably he, like Siemiatkowski, agreed that current financial institutions lacked the innovative spirit to introduce this type of payment option. So, undaunted by their loss in the competition, the three entrepreneurs found sufficient courage to continue.

They quickly converted their company — then called Kreditor — from concept to reality. And at 11:06 a.m. on April 10, 2005, the first payment using their technology was made at Pocketklubben, a Swedish bookstore.

From there, the company expanded fast. In 2010, the name changed to Klarna — Swedish for "transparent." By then, its success really was clear; and in 2012, it achieved unicorn status — tech-talk for a valuation of $1 billion or more.[56]

Fast forward to today, and Klarna is a fully licensed bank serving 93 million customers worldwide.[57] It now has 600,000 retail partners that benefit from 2.5 million purchases via Klarna every day — and is valued at $15 billion.[58]

And all because the concept is so effective. Research by management consultancy firm Bain[59] has revealed that almost 60% of shops that offered their customers a "buy now, pay later" option saw a boost to their conversion rates. Additionally, 47% saw an increase in average order value.

Why does it work? There are two key elements to Klarna: the ability to defer payment for, say, 30 days and the opportunity to split the cost over multiple payments. Both features tend to make customers less price sensitive, and thus more inclined to complete their purchases and buy more.

Let's look at the behavioral science principles they're using.

In the here and now

The most important bias at work for Klarna is *present bias*. This means we tend to give stronger weight to payoffs in the here and now, rather than equivalent or even higher payoffs in the future.

So, if a clothing store charges us $50 for a sweater and we need to pay today, it feels painful. But if we have to pay in a month's time, well, that hurts less. We underestimate the discomfort of future payment, because we're pretty bad at imagining how we'll feel in a few weeks' time.

> We tend to give stronger weight to payoffs in the here and now, rather than equivalent or even higher payoffs in the future.

The term present bias has been in use since the 1960s and there's solid experimental evidence to support it. One such study was conducted in 2017 by Liam Delaney and Leonhard Lades at the University of Stirling. They gave 144 participants a hypothetical purchase scenario, in which they were asked to decide between making an immediate smaller payment (£9–£15) or a larger, future one (£16).

The researchers discovered that, rather than pay £13 immediately, 60% chose to pay £16 in one month's time. This equates to a 23% monthly interest rate or an APR of 1099% — not a rational financial choice. This illustrates that we're far more influenced by costs in the present than equivalent costs in the future.

But this thought experiment is pretty abstract. And we know that what people say they would do and what they actually do can be quite different. However, there's evidence from the real world to suggest that present bias is a genuine finding. In a 2011 study, Anna Breman of the Stockholm School of Economics worked with a large Swedish charity called Diakonia to explore the phenomenon.

The experiment involved 1,134 regular donors. Half were asked to increase their contributions immediately. The other half were asked if they would agree to increase their donations in two months' time.

The results were impressive. First, the delayed givers were 11% more likely to agree to increase their regular donations. Second, the upgrades they made were larger. The average increase was 72 Swedish krona compared to 61 among the control group — a 19% difference. Overall, this resulted in 32% more in contributions; just by pushing the request a couple of months into the future.

The combination of Delaney's research, Breman's experiment and many other similar studies should give you faith in this insight.

Evolutionary roots

There appears to be an evolutionary rationale for present bias. Thousands of years ago, when we lived in hunter-gatherer groups, our most pressing survival needs were immediate ones: eating and drinking. There was a high degree of uncertainty as to when our next meal would appear. So, if food was on offer right now, we would most definitely accept it. Longer-term future events were irrelevant if we couldn't survive long enough to have a future.

Of course, the situation is very different today. Food is plentiful, and if we turn down a donut now, we can be confident of getting hold of something tasty later. But these deep-seated biases evolved millennia ago. Our food circumstances have improved much faster than the human brain could evolve. So, the bias towards the present moment is strong, mismatched as it may be to modern life. Our impatience is hardwired.

Applying present bias

Aligning with present bias in business can be simple. First, and most obviously, there are plenty of e-commerce applications. Do what you can to push costs for your customers into the future. This might include tactics such as introductory offers, stepping up fees over time or payment delays. And services such as Klarna, or similar brands like Afterpay, make this easy to do. The evidence shows it'll be well worth it.

Second, there will be occasions when you need to tell customers about a price increase. Leveraging present bias, you can soften the blow by giving them as much notice as possible. If you tell customers about a $10 hike in next month's bill, it will aggravate them. But tell them about a rise in the distant future — say, three or six months away — and it'll feel far less meaningful, less unpleasant and more forgivable.

Playing with time

Moving payment into the future is not the only element of Klarna that reduces price sensitivity. Another feature is the ability to split your payments into smaller parts. This taps into an idea called *temporal reframing*, also known as the *pennies-a-day effect*.

The original study demonstrating this was conducted in 1998 by John Gourville at Harvard University. He showed 120 participants one of six hypothetical charity donation requests. The requests were presented as either:

- a daily figure ($1 a day for a year); or
- an annual figure, almost equivalent ($350 per year).

The findings were clear: participants were 53% more likely to agree to the $1 request than the annual one — even though the yearly amount was $15 smaller.

Why does this happen? The most likely explanation is that people consider the specific amount being sought and imagine what else they could do with that money. So, when a dollar is mentioned, they might picture a can of soda. Crucially, they think of a single can — rather than doing the math and picturing 365 cans.

The question then becomes whether helping to feed a hungry child, and the accompanying warm glow, means more than a can of Coke. The answer, most likely, is yes.

But, the annual amount conjures a different image. If you think of $350, what springs to mind? A winter coat? A night in a nice hotel? A meal out with the family? That feels like a more sizable sacrifice, and one that may give you pause when deciding whether to donate.

Gourville's findings are interesting but, again, related to charity donations. However, in 2015 Richard ran a study to explore the pennies-a-day effect in a commercial setting.

He showed 500 people an ad featuring an image of a sports car, with a brief description. Each ad also included the price, but participants saw the amount expressed as either a daily, weekly, monthly, or yearly sum.

Participants were asked to judge whether the car represented good value. The results are shown in Table 14 and the figures relate to the percentage of people who thought the car was a good or great deal.

Table 14: Prices expressed over a shorter period appear better value

PRICE PER	PRICE SHOWN	PERCENTAGE THINKING CAR WAS "GOOD" OR "GREAT" VALUE
Year	£1,668	11%
Month	£139	40%
Week	£32	43%
Day	£4.57	51%

~5X

Source: Adapted from Shotton (2015).

The results revealed that the longer the timeframe, the less appealing the deal. With the price listed as an annual amount, 11% saw it as a great deal. When expressed as a daily sum, this increased almost fivefold: more than half of people rated the deal as great.

In 2022, we set out to explore the concept further. This time, we wanted to see whether framing costs on a per-unit basis would have a similar effect to temporal reframing.

We asked 282 consumers to imagine they saw Sierra Nevada Pale Ale for sale in a supermarket. We told half the participants that the ale cost $18.99 for 12 330ml bottles.

However, we gave the other half an additional piece of information: the $18.99 was equivalent to $1.58 a bottle. People were then asked whether the price represented good value.

The results showed that people who saw the per-unit equivalent were more than twice as likely to think that the ale was quite good or very good value compared to those who were only presented with the whole sum (28.6% vs 13.7%).

Applying price framing

There are a few simple steps that brands can take to boost customers' willingness to pay based on temporal and unit reframing.

Your customers have a strong tendency to place undue importance on the headline number, neglecting the fact that smaller units over time might add up to a larger total. And they'd rather avoid anything that feels like a return to school arithmetic.

You can harness this by allowing customers to spread cost over time — through Klarna, for example — and ensuring you present your prices using the smallest sums you can. That might involve reframing the whole price as a certain amount per day or week; or it could be cost per item if you're offering multipacks. Consider how you can show customers the smallest possible number.

THREE KEY TAKEAWAYS

1. **Be mindful of timing**: People are more interested in costs and benefits in the immediate term than in the future. Structure your pricing to reflect that.

2. **Use the pennies-a-day effect**: Your customers won't automatically slice and dice your price into all possible permutations. So do it for them. If you sell your products on a time basis, communicate your prices using the smallest time length you can. Talk about the price of your service per day, not per year.

3. **Break your prices down to the unit price**: If you don't have a time-based product you can still apply the same basic principle. You can make prices appear lower by illustrating the cost on a per unit basis. So, if you're selling beer, talk about the per bottle cost as well as the case price.

14

GOT MILK?

AT THE MENTION of cookies, does your mind immediately turn to milk?

There's a high chance it does. And this insight lies at the heart of one of advertising's greatest success stories: the iconic "Got Milk?" campaign.

Let's take a look at the behavioral science behind the triumph that stopped milk sales turning sour and grew to become part of US popular culture.

Boosting 'milk drunk' not 'milk drinkers'

In 1993, milk consumption in California was in decline. According to the strangely named California Fluid Milk Processors' Advisory Board (CFMPAB) something had to be done.

Recent ads had managed to shift attitudes to milk, painting it as wholesome and "Good for You." But this wasn't translating into sales.

Which is how executive director of CFMPAB Jim Manning came to approach ad agency Goodby, Silverstein & Partners with a new brief. Manning said: "I'm not interested in image. We need to affect behavior… That's the objective. And I don't give a damn how we get there." An exciting prospect for any creative.

The agency's first insight was that 70% of people were already consuming milk — a good place to start.[60] So, the team agreed to focus on a change in the degree of milk-drinking behavior among the majority, rather than the adoption of a new behavior in the few.

They began exploring exactly how milk drinkers felt about it. How did they use it? A tracking survey revealed that 88% of milk was consumed in the home.[61] And crucially, this was because it was almost always a "companion" to something else.

From this insight grew a conviction that these companion foods should be used in the advertising. The agency set up focus groups to explore the idea.

Support group or focus group?

Here's the lovely creative part of the story: the agency asked a group of participants to avoid consuming any milk for a week before they met, offering an extra financial incentive if they agreed. They were requested to keep a diary during their milk-free week, listing everything they'd eaten and drunk, plus what they were doing and how they felt at the time.

It turned out that the hunch around companion foods was spot on — people really missed milk when they couldn't have it. The research generated some unexpectedly impassioned responses.

One woman described an awful day, with conflict at work and a crappy commute. She'd bought herself a couple of cookies to enjoy once she got home. Finally, with the kids in bed, she sat down to enjoy her snack in front of the TV. When she realized she would not be allowed the milk to go with them, it was the last straw: "It was awful. I thought about lying to the focus group... but then I put the milk back. And the cookies just weren't the same. It was a bad end to a bad day."

Her testimonial, according to agency planner Jon Steel, turned the focus group into a kind of milk deprivation support group. There was an outpouring of frustration as everyone agreed that the last week had reminded them of other unhappy occasions when they'd run out of milk.[62] Because, as Manning put it: "Nothing else except milk works. Soda doesn't work, Gatorade doesn't work, water doesn't work. The only thing that works in that bowl of Cheerios is milk."[63]

The insights gathered from these focus groups led to an evolution of the companion foods idea, with a subtle shift away from "milk and..." to "no milk and..." The idea was to evoke the sense of deprivation felt when there's no milk to go with your cookies, your coffee, or your morning cereal.

The creatives decided to run with this and came up with a simple yet genius tagline that captured the impact of running out of milk: "Got Milk?" The campaign took off from there, with a series of now-legendary ads.

The first TV commercial, "Aaron Burr," is perhaps one of the best known. It opens on a history geek surrounded by Alexander Hamilton memorabilia, listening to classical radio and spreading peanut butter onto bread. The music ends and the radio announcer moves onto the quiz slot, with the question: "Who shot Alexander Hamilton in that famous duel?" The geek's phone rings: it's the radio host calling him live on air, with the chance to win $10,000 if he can answer the question. He can, of course! Alexander Hamilton is his passion; he's been waiting for this opportunity his whole life. And he correctly answers, "Aaron Burr." But — oh no! His mouth is so stuffed with sticky peanut butter that his reply is muffled. He reaches for some milk to help him swallow — the carton is empty! He just can't get the answer out clearly. The radio host doesn't catch what he's saying and bang — there goes that $10,000 prize.

Why were the ad, and the campaign that followed, so powerful?

It's what you *don't* have that matters

Running out of milk cost the poor guy in the commercial $10,000. This ad, and a whole campaign of others, reminds us of that heart-sinking moment when you realize there's no milk. Maybe you've already poured a bowl of your favorite cereal, brewed a coffee, or served up some freshly baked cookies — then opened the fridge only to discover you won't get to enjoy your treat after all.

The sense of deprivation is powerful, and that's because at its foundation lies the bias of *loss aversion*.

This is the idea that loss looms much larger in our minds than equivalent gains. If that feels a bit abstract, an example might help. Imagine: you're walking home one evening and you spot a crisp $5 bill on the sidewalk. Noticing it will give you a small jolt of happiness.

But someone else is about to discover they have lost $5 and when they do it'll create a greater degree of unhappiness. Even though the sums are the same for each person, the impact is different. That's loss aversion.

> Loss looms much larger in our minds than equivalent gains.

This bias was first described by Israeli psychologists Amos Tversky and Daniel Kahneman in 1979. In their experiment, the psychologists offered people a bet on a coin flip: tails, they lose and have to hand over $10; heads, they win.

The researchers wanted to know the amount people would need to be offered as a win before they took the bet. The key finding was that most people wouldn't gamble unless they were set to win at least $20 — they'd rather not risk losing $10 unless the potential reward was double that.

Other studies have shown a similar effect in real-world situations. For example, in 1988, psychologist Marti Hope Gonzales

CHAPTER 14: GOT MILK?

and colleagues at the University of Minnesota, conducted an experiment into the effects of loss aversion on energy conservation.

An official from a local energy company offered 404 homeowners an audit, which gave them the option of insulating their homes. Half of the homeowners were told that if they insulated their homes, they would be able to **save** $0.75 a day. The other half were told that if they failed to insulate their homes, they would **lose** $0.75 a day.

This apparently minor tweak in wording had a considerable effect. Of the homeowners who were simply told what they could save, just 39% opted for the energy saving initiative. Of those told what they could lose, 61% took up the offer. That's a difference of 56%. Exactly the same financial incentive had a markedly different effect depending on how it was framed.

So, we're powerfully motivated by a wish to avoid losing out on something. It's a fact that could be applied more frequently in marketing. Most brands communicate what you'll gain if you buy them. Influential? Potentially. But loss aversion suggests telling people what they'll miss out on if they don't purchase will be more effective.

For example, if you work for a broadband provider, rather than say "Switch to us and save $100," try "If you don't switch to us, you'll be wasting $100."

Or perhaps you want your customers to use web chat rather than call. Don't tell them they'll save time, instead say it helps them stop wasting time. They're simple copy tweaks, but ones that have a significant effect.

But with "Got Milk?" loss aversion is used more subtly. The campaign didn't use explicit wording; it generated a feeling of loss. The TV ads effectively evoked the sense of frustration and disappointment, shared in the focus group, that we feel when we've been looking forward to something and then it falls through. Rather than reminding us how good things like Oreos and Trix are with milk, it's about how awful life is without them. A much stronger sensation.

Brands should take note of this subtle usage: implying loss aversion opens up multiple opportunities. Take a look at the example below. It's from an imaginary brand, Buffle's Car Wash, and offers three packages, each at a different price point.

Many brands in this situation would detail the benefits of each package, with a growing list for the more premium offerings. However, Buffle's does something slightly different: note the crosses. It explicitly highlights what you'll lose out on if you go for the cheaper options. That's a simple application of loss aversion.

Figure 9: Implied loss aversion in action at Buffle's car wash

BUFFLE'S CAR WASH	STANDARD $15	STANDARD+ $20	PREMIUM $25
EXTERIOR WASH	✓	✓	✓
AIR DRY	✓	✓	✓
WHEEL & TIRE RINSE	✓	✓	✓
WINDOW CLEANING	✗	✓	✓
INTERIOR VACUUM	✗	✓	✓
TIRE SHINE	✗	✗	✓
TRIPLE FOAM CONDITIONER	✗	✗	✓

Source: Myroshnychenko (2025).

CHAPTER 14: GOT MILK?

Who said or what said?

In 1995, the new milk ads went national. The Milk Processor Education Program decided it was time to get on board with "Got Milk?" Enlisting the help of another agency, Bozell, it took the idea in a new direction and came up with the milk mustache campaign.

Here, a different tactic helped to cement "Got Milk?" as a national household catchphrase. The agency recruited a host of celebrities to endorse the campaign, including some seriously A-list names, such as Bill Clinton, Elton John, Beyoncé, Michael Jordan, and many more.

The use of celebrity endorsements was huge at the time: just think Michael Jordan × Nike, Tom Cruise × Ray-Ban, Michael Jackson × Pepsi... the list goes on. Some of these celebrities created a fortune for the brands they worked with.

But why are they so effective? Influencer endorsement is based on a bias called the *messenger effect*, which describes how we are strongly influenced by *who* communicates information.

One classic study demonstrating this was conducted in 1951 by Carl Hovland and Walter Weiss at Yale University. They asked 223 participants to indicate their stance on one of four subjects. Questions related to topical issues — for example, "Can a practicable atomic-powered submarine be built at the present time?" Participants gave their initial opinion on the question and then, five days later, were given an article on the subject laying out a counterargument to their opinion.

> We are strongly influenced by *who* communicates information.

Each participant saw the same article for a given topic. The twist in the experiment was that some were told the piece came from a high-credibility source, and others that it was from a low-credibility source. In the case of the atomic submarine question, for example, the article was said to come from either physicist Robert Oppenheimer or *Pravda* (a Soviet newspaper).

Participants were then asked if they had changed their minds. The results were striking. Even though everyone had received exactly the same information, when they believed it came from a low-credibility messenger, just 7% changed their minds on the question; but when they thought they were hearing the counterargument from a high-credibility source, 23% switched viewpoints. That's more than a threefold difference.

Brands normally focus on what they say. However, the messenger effect suggests that you should focus just as much on *who* communicates the message.

The effect is also seen among experts in their fields, who you might expect to only be swayed by the message itself. In a 2023 study, Mohsen Javdani at Simon Fraser University and Ha-Joon Chang at Cambridge University examined the effects of message source on 2,245 economists from 19 different countries.

These participants were shown statements written by prominent economists. The same statements were attributed to either a respected economics source or a less well-known, non-mainstream source. Participants were then asked to indicate how much they agreed with the statements.

The researchers found that changing the message source from respected economists to lesser known ones reduced agreement by 7.3%. This clearly demonstrates that the source of a message can unconsciously influence how we interpret information, even among experts.

Interestingly, when asked, 82% of the economists said that they based their evaluations solely on the content of the statements. Yet again, this highlights the gap between what people think influences them and what actually does.

CHAPTER 14: GOT MILK?

So, applying the messenger effect and using well-known, much-loved faces to deliver your message would seem an effective strategic approach for brands — and there's no doubt that it worked for "Got Milk?"

There's more than just anecdotal evidence that the messenger effect works well for brands. In 2017, Johannes Knoll and Jörg Matthes from the University of Vienna conducted a meta-analysis examining the effectiveness of celebrity endorsements on brand perception.

They reviewed 46 studies and found that celebrity endorsements increased positive attitudes toward the ad and the product. Interestingly, actors seem to have the strongest effect, so people like Harrison Ford, Noah Wyle, Jennifer Love Hewitt, Lindsay Lohan, Jennifer Aniston, and Lisa Kudrow — all at the height of their fame in the 1990s — were likely to have been particularly impactful in the "Got Milk?" campaign.

So, if you're hankering after milk and cookies now, the reasons may be rooted in behavioral science as much as your love of the white stuff.

THREE KEY TAKEAWAYS

1. **Fear of loss is a serious motivator**: Most brands communicate what shoppers will gain by buying them. But since losses motivate people more than the equivalent gain, this approach should be flipped on its head. Instead, tell consumers what they stand to miss out on if they don't buy your product.

2. **Apply the biases creatively**: Don't feel hamstrung by the experiments. If you apply them with creative license you'll have the biggest impact.

3. **Find the best messenger**: Who says something is as important as what is said. Rather than singing your own praises as a brand, get someone else to do it.

15

KENTUCKY FRIED CHICKEN

Fancy a fast-food hit? Chances are you won't be far from a KFC. The brand is still going strong more than 90 years after Colonel Sanders first started selling fried chicken from his own kitchen.

But what is the secret to its success? Well, "secret" is the operative word.

Off to a late start

It wasn't until age 40, after a string of failed careers, that Sanders finally landed in the food industry. He was offered a gas station in Corbin, Kentucky, in return for a percentage of sales. With a canny eye for an opportunity, he started offering hot meals to drivers passing down Route 25.

To begin with, he cooked up dishes in his own kitchen and seated customers around his own table. Word got out about the tasty fare and he expanded into a cafe — which did well enough to be listed in the 1939 *Adventures in Good Eating* restaurant guide. "Sanders Court and Cafè" was on the map.

Sanders always served chicken, but it took a while longer to land on the idea of pressure frying, and to perfect a seasoning featuring 11 herbs and spices. He kept this recipe a well-guarded secret.

In the 1950s, Sanders began using his status as a Kentucky colonel to develop a unique brand, dressing up in a frock coat and string tie. Within a few years, there were 200 franchised restaurants and the Kentucky Fried Chicken brand was competing with hamburgers as America's favorite fast food of the day.[64]

Since then, KFC has thrived. Now owned by Yum! Brands, there are over 30,000 KFC outlets worldwide[65] serving fried chicken to an estimated 12 million people every day.[66]

Apart from a great founder's story, what's the secret to its success?

Shh: keep the secret

Ever since its beginnings, an air of mystery has surrounded Colonel Sanders' KFC recipe. Even today, it remains a closely kept secret. The seasoning blend has never been patented — a deliberate decision, because patents are public and eventually expire.

The brand has gone to some lengths to retain the mystique. It's reported that half of the spice mix is made by one manufacturer, which passes this on to another manufacturer to add the rest of the ingredients — no single company has the full recipe.

The KFC spice mix has secured almost legendary status. Rumor has it that a copy of the recipe exists in a safe at the KFC headquarters in Louisville, alongside 11 vials of herbs and spices. Another story in circulation is that only two people in the world know the full recipe, and they're not allowed to travel on a plane together.

It's entirely possible that the recipe is now out there in the public domain, and that a search online will reveal the truth. But how can you be sure that what you find will be genuine?

This veil of secrecy that surrounds the recipe is one of the elements that attracts consumers.

Information gap

With KFC's secret recipe, we know there is something to know, but we don't know what that something is. That's what George Loewenstein, a psychologist at Carnegie Mellon, calls an *information gap*. And it's this that piques our interest. In Loewenstein's words, curiosity occurs when "there is a discrepancy between what one knows and what one wishes to know."

Jonah Lehrer puts it more poetically. He says an information gap is a "mental itch, a mosquito bite on the brain." In the case of KFC, our minds may well be driven to taste the food in an attempt to scratch that itch.

There's evidence for this phenomenon. In 1994, Loewenstein and his colleagues at Carnegie Mellon recruited a group of participants and split them in two. Each group saw a computer screen featuring a grid made up of squares. Next, all respondents were asked to click on at least five squares to reveal an image. Crucially, there was a slight delay — they had to wait four seconds before selecting the next square.

In the first group, each time participants clicked on a square, they saw a different animal. The image was complete — a whole horse, a whole wolf. No mystery involved. You can see a mock-up of what these participants might have seen after selecting two squares.

However, in the second group, each click revealed just part of an animal — a flank, or a bit of hind leg, say. They were pieces of a puzzle. Have a look at figure 11 and you can see what they'd have been shown.

Figure 10: A grid with complete images

Source: Adapted from Loewenstein (1994).

Figure 11: A grid with incomplete images

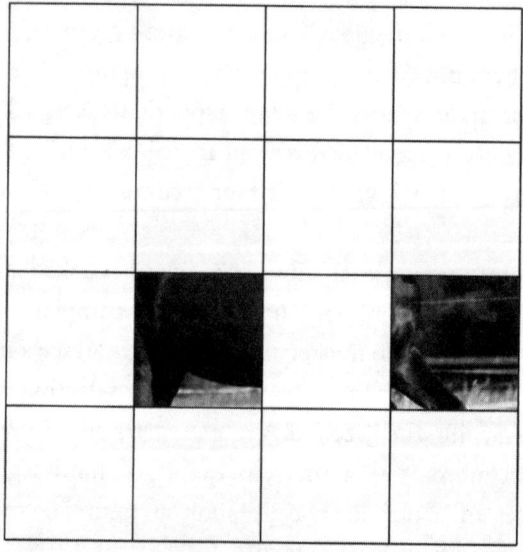

Source: Adapted from Loewenstein (1994).

CHAPTER 15: KENTUCKY FRIED CHICKEN

And the researchers found something interesting — group two clicked on substantially more squares than group one, even though they were only required to pick five, and clicking any more required additional time and patience.

According to Loewenstein's information gap theory, this was because participants in the second group were curious to solve the puzzle and reveal the hidden animal. Conversely, participants in the first group were less curious, since every image contained a complete animal.

Our desire to close these information gaps is hardwired. There's an evolutionary advantage to inquisitiveness; those who wanted to find out more were better placed to survive and therefore pass on their genes.

> Those who wanted to find out more were better placed to survive and therefore pass on their genes.

Crucially, though, Loewenstein's study shows that it's not just life-saving mysteries that enthrall us. Even the most mundane information gaps — like what animal might be behind these squares, or what are those secret 11 herbs and spices — get us craving to know more. In the psychologist's words, "There is a natural inclination to resolve information gaps, even for questions of no importance."

Once KFC's mystery has sparked our interest, we might also reflect that the lengths they go to keep the recipe secret insinuates that it must be special. Surely only someone in ownership of a highly valuable, sought after recipe would go through such rigmarole for so many years to guard it?

An unsolved mystery

But secrets stoke more than just interest. The fact that the mystery isn't resolved also makes it more memorable. It does so by tapping into a powerful bias known as the *Zeigarnik effect*, named after the Soviet psychologist who first described it.

Bluma Zeigarnik was supposedly inspired to research this phenomenon after a fateful trip to a cafe in 1927 with her University of Berlin mentor, Kurt Lewin, and a group of fellow students. They placed a lengthy order of food and drinks, which the waiter listened to without writing anything down. A few minutes later, their order arrived without fault: an impressive performance.

After settling the bill and leaving the restaurant, Zeigarnik realized she had left her scarf behind. She returned and, with relief, spotted her waiter, whose memory was so strong that he'd surely be able to help. But when she asked him if he'd seen her scarf, he looked perplexed. He didn't even recognize her.

Zeigarnik was intrigued. How could someone who had performed such an impressive feat of recall then fail to remember her? She began to wonder if there is a fundamental difference between how our minds deal with completed and uncompleted tasks.

To test her hypothesis, she carried out a study in which she gave people a series of challenges such as solving puzzles or assembling a cardboard box. Half the participants were allowed to complete the task, while the others were stopped halfway through. She later questioned participants about the details of the process.

The results revealed that those who had been interrupted were able to recall 90% more detail than those who had completed the task.

But why does this effect occur? Well, we live in a world of excess information and we don't have the capacity to remember everything. There has to be a degree of selection. We have to focus on what matters. And one rule of thumb used for prioritization is whether

CHAPTER 15: KENTUCKY FRIED CHICKEN

a task has been completed or not. Arguably, once completed, the information becomes less valuable and can therefore be discarded.

In the case of the impressive waiter, during the ordering process, the task was ongoing and the details of the meal had to be recalled until after serving. But once the guests had left, serving that group was a ticked-off task and could be forgotten.

Zeigarnik's study is interesting, but you might wonder whether experiments involving puzzles apply to advertising. However, there's evidence that her findings can be confidently extrapolated. In 1972, Jacob Jacoby from Purdue University and James Heimbach from the Nationwide Research Center showed participants a 30-minute TV program interspersed with ads. The six ads were either complete, cut off at the beginning or cut at the end. Afterwards, participants were asked to name the brand and describe the ad.

> Once completed, the information becomes less valuable and can therefore be discarded.

Immediate recall of the unfinished ads was 34% greater than when they were watched right through, and 52% greater when participants were asked to recall the brands two days later.

Together, the information gap theory and Zeigarnik effect explain some of the power of KFC's secret recipe. We are intrigued by an unsolved mystery. It stays with us: we keep wondering what really goes into the herb and spice mix. Wise to this, KFC's campaigns continually reminds us that we don't know, and in so doing, keeps the brand front of mind.

So, think about your product. Can you create allure and memorability by holding back information about how it was created? Is there a secret element that you could draw attention to? Just make sure to tell people there's a mystery. Only then have you set up an information gap and tapped into the Zeigarnik effect.

Or perhaps you could take inspiration from a smaller-scale example of secrecy that KFC employs. In 2020, in Australia, it created a "secret menu" of staff specials, which could only be accessed by following a particular sequence of navigations on the app. When it launched, KFC kept quiet, waited for someone to notice and then let social media do the rest. It was an incredible success, with a 111% increase in app downloads and customers spending 77% more on the secret menu.[67]

An unsolved mystery is something we find hard to ignore. That's the beauty of it — and the reason why these tactics are so impactful and memorable.

A question of supply and demand?

So far, we've discussed how KFC boosts demand by restricting information about its recipe. But that's not the only restriction it applies; another tactic is to impose limits on how much people can buy. Paradoxically, this boosts demand.

The idea of scarcity stimulating demand is a fundamental principle of behavioral science. It's one that brands can easily exploit, as shown by a 2012 study by Seung Yun Lee from Hanyang University in South Korea.

He gave participants an ad for a wristwatch. Half saw an ad featuring a scarcity message such as, "Exclusive limited edition. Hurry, limited stocks." The other half saw messaging that emphasized the large number of items available, such as "New edition. Many items in stock." Participants indicated their purchase intent on a nine-point scale (one = not at all likely; nine = very likely).

The message communicating plentiful supply resulted in a purchase intent rating of 3.37, whereas those who saw the scarcity messaging rated their likelihood to purchase as 4.62 — that's a 37% increase. Scarcity produced a strong effect.

CHAPTER 15: KENTUCKY FRIED CHICKEN

In fact, scarcity is one of the biases that holds the greatest sway in decision-making. Support for its impact as a marketing tool comes from a 2017 review by Will Browne and Mike Swarbrick Jones at Qubit Digital. They analyzed 6,700 e-commerce campaigns and found that scarcity was one of the best ways to boost sales.

Messages highlighting scarcity resulted in an average 2.9% uplift — this was the highest impact among the 29 message types tested. The third highest was urgency, or time scarcity, which resulted in a 1.5% increase in sales.

Table 15: Scarcity was the most effective of 29 message types tested (measured by uplift in revenue per visitor)

TREATMENT	UPLIFT
Scarcity	2.9%
Social proof	2.3%
Urgency (Time scarcity)	1.5%
Abandonment	1.1%
Product recommendations	0.4%

Source: Adapted from Browne & Swarbrick Jones (2017).

Scarcity is an easy tactic to apply: you simply highlight your limited supply to stimulate greater interest among your customers. But there's another way, which doesn't require any actual shortage — and that's the approach taken by KFC.

We want what we (think we) can't have

If you'd stepped into a KFC in Australia in 2016, you might have seen an offer for $1 AUD fries. Posters featured a mouthwatering image of a large serving in KFC's iconic red and white packaging emblazoned with Colonel Sanders' face.

Sounds like an OK offer, right?

But there was an extra line beneath the amazing price: "max four per person."

Chances are, you'd be tempted to make a purchase.

Why? Because of scarcity. The fewer we can have, the more we want. There isn't really a shortage of KFC fries, but limiting the maximum number of purchases per customer gives the impression that there may be. To customers, it appears that the fries are such good value, KFC can't afford to sell too many. This is an idea called *false scarcity*.

Some evidence of the impact of false scarcity comes from a 1998 study by Brian Wansink, a professor of marketing at Cornell University.[68] He ran a field experiment to test the effectiveness of the false scarcity tactic.

He persuaded three supermarkets in Sioux City, Iowa, to offer Campbell's soup at a small discount: $0.79 rather than $0.89. He asked the store to sell the discounted soup in three conditions:

- Control with no limit on the number of purchases;
- Test one: customers limited to four cans;
- Test two: customers limited to 12 cans.

In the unlimited condition, shoppers bought 3.3 cans on average. When the cap was four cans, they bought slightly more — 3.5. And when the limit was 12 cans, they bought an average of seven cans.

The final condition works best because in addition to scarcity,

CHAPTER 15: KENTUCKY FRIED CHICKEN

the limit becomes an anchor number and customers adjust their purchasing behavior in relation to the quoted figure.

Curious to discover if the finding was genuine, we conducted another false scarcity experiment.

We recruited 282 US respondents and assigned them to one of two groups. The control group, who were told to imagine they saw a case of beer on sale for $18.99. The false scarcity group were given the same price, but also informed that they could buy a maximum of six cases. Both groups were then asked whether they thought the offer represented good value.

Among those in the control group, 13.7% regarded the offer as quite good or very good value. In the false scarcity group, this figure was 21.8% — that's a 59% difference.

This evidence shows why KFC's approach worked. And the sales data backs this up: sales of $1 AUD chips increased by 56% versus the same period the previous year.[69] There was also an increase in the number of customers who bought four packets of $1 AUD chips: 87% versus 29% previously.

Customers believed the price was good value, and were clearly tempted to buy more than they otherwise might have.

Next time you run a promotion, emulate KFC by limiting the number of items people can buy per visit. People will assume it's either such a good deal that it's a genuine loss leader or that the price is so appealing you're worried it might sell out. Either way it'll boost the demand.

THREE KEY TAKEAWAYS

1. **Lean into the mystery**: Your customers will remember what is unfinished. So retaining a degree of secrecy or mystery around your product will help to keep your brand front of mind.
2. **Create desire through scarcity**: We want what we can't have. Communicating scarcity is one of the most effective ways of boosting demand. Emphasize either the small volume of products available or the short window of time people have to act.
3. **Limits can drive demand**: Limiting the number of items that customers can purchase per visit is a simple way to apply scarcity.

16

PRINGLES

"**O**NCE YOU POP, you can't stop" — a genius strapline. Almost anyone on the street could tell you the brand. It's a global snack phenomenon; but what are the behavioral insights that fed Pringles' success?

Chip, crisp or what?

During the Second World War, eating became pretty boring. When rationing ended in the late 1940s, people embraced snacks again — including chips, now that they were back on offer. But customers weren't satisfied with the oily crumbs available.

In 1956, Procter & Gamble (P&G) set out to put that right. The company employed chemist Frank Baur to come up with something that wouldn't crumble in the bag. Baur used his math knowhow to come up with a whole new concept: a saddle-shaped snack designed to be packaged safely in a tube and stay whole.

This novel product, called Pringles Newfangled Potato Chips, met the brief for a chip that wouldn't fall apart and leave your fingers greasy. However, it didn't take off — because Baur had failed to factor in the importance of flavor. Yes, the chips held their shape; but they didn't taste good.

So, it was back to the drawing board. P&G brought in a new researcher to develop Baur's work and a fresh Pringles recipe was patented.

Stories abound about the derivation of the brand name. Was it because of a street in Ohio — Pringle Drive — where two P&G ad execs lived? Is it a kind of distorted portmanteau of the parent company name? A researcher named Mark Pringle is reportedly listed on the patent application — was it down to him? Nobody knows.

When the product relaunched with the new recipe, its reception was far more positive. The packaging featured a jolly-looking mustachioed man, apparently named Julius Pringle.

The campaign was going well until snack-making competitors complained about the use of the word "chip." The complaint was upheld, and in 1975 the Food and Drug Administration ruled that Pringles should be called "crisps." According to their definition, a chip should be made from a slice of potato and should not contain large amounts of other carbohydrate types, which Pringles most definitely do.

But the fact that they're made from a mix of dried potato, rice flour, cornstarch, and wheat starch has in no way dented their popularity. Pringles is now the third most popular brand of US potato snack, after Lay's and Ruffles, with a 13% share of the market.[70]

There's a huge range of flavors available, which vary by market. In Japan, seaweed flavor is popular; in South Korea, mayo cheese goes down well. The brand generates annual revenues of $3 billion,[71] according to parent company Kellanova, and Julius Pringle has come to be one of the world's most recognizable brand mascots.

The novel shape of both the snack and the packaging has surely had something to do with its success. Who hasn't got their hand jammed in a tube at some point? Or made a duck's bill from two crisps? Or maybe even tried to build a Pringle ring? Baur was so proud of his creation that he reportedly requested to have some of his ashes buried in a Pringle tube when he died.

So, which biases helped the Pringles brand to become the snack icon it is today?

Words that stick, rhymes that click

No prizes for guessing where we start. "Once you pop, you can't stop" — it just rings true doesn't it? Pringles are fiendishly moreish. Of course, it's not true — in fact, more so than with any other chip brand, you can stop when you want, replace the lid, and still keep the chips fresh.

But the slogan seems to give you permission to go ahead and chomp through the whole tube. Why do we believe it? It's a bias called the *Keats heuristic*, which suggests that we trust rhyming phrases more than non-rhyming ones. Psychologists think this happens because rhymes improve reading flow, making a sentence easier for our brains to process. And we equate ease of processing with truth.

> We trust rhyming phrases more than non-rhyming ones.

Evidence of this comes from a study conducted in 1999 by psychologists Matthew McGlone and Jessica Tofighbakhsh from Lafayette College, Pennsylvania. They split participants into two groups and gave each group a list of lesser-known proverbs. For one group, these were in their natural rhyming form; for the other group, the proverbs were adjusted so that they had the same meaning but didn't rhyme. Here are some examples:

Table 16: The phrases used in the Keats heuristic study

RHYMING VERSION	NON-RHYMING VERSION
Woes unite foes	Woes unite enemies
Anger restrained is wisdom gained	Anger held back is wisdom gained
Those who are poor by condition are rich in ambition	Those who are poor by circumstance are rich in ambition
What sobriety conceals, alcohol reveals	What sobriety conceals, alcohol unmasks

Source: Adapted from McGlone and Tofighbakhsh (1999).

The results showed that the rhyming versions were 17% more likely to be considered true than their non-rhyming alternatives.

It's something that Pringles has long made use of — as far back as the 1980s and 1990s, the brand has favored a rhyme. In the infamous ad that Brad Pitt might wish we'd all forget, the slogan was "The fever reliever." We've also had "No-drip, no-dip, 3-layer snack." And in the 2000s, they used "Snack stacks — what would you do to put that crunch in your lunch?" It's a trick that works amazingly well. Because a rhyme not only boosts believability (note how the ad suggesting we eat Pringles in a stack of three seems reasonable?), but also makes it much easier to remember a phrase. "Once you take the lid off, you can't stop" simply wouldn't ring true and would not stick in our minds.

The connection between rhyming and memorability is used intuitively in advertising, but it also has a solid evidence base. For example, Petra Filkuková of the University of Oslo and Sven Hroar Klempe of the Norwegian University of Science and Technology demonstrated this in a 2013 study.

To get closer to a genuine commercial setting, the researchers used real brands, such as clothes brand EGO and a diet course called BetterLife. They generated slogans for these brands that either rhymed or didn't. They then recruited 183 participants and showed them nine slogans, with half the group seeing rhyming versions and the other half non-rhyming alternatives. Respondents rated the slogans on a range of measures.

The results showed that when the slogans rhymed, there was a 25% increase in memorability versus the non-rhyming versions. Interestingly, the rhyming versions performed significantly higher on a number of other metrics too, including likability (24% higher), trustworthiness (22% higher), and persuasiveness (21% higher).

We wanted to test these findings ourselves, so in 2024 we ran an experiment with Jon Puleston and Nicki Morley at Kantar. We showed 401 nationally representative participants a list of ten statements, half of which rhymed and half of which didn't. Respondents were later asked to list as many of the phrases as possible.

The results were conclusive. Participants were more than three and a half times as likely to remember a rhyming phrase than a non-rhyming one.

It's a strategy that has been used to great success by iconic brands such as Haribo ("Kids and grown ups love it so, the happy world of Haribo"), 7 Eleven ("Oh, thank heaven for 7 Eleven"), and Mars ("A Mars a day helps you work, rest and play"). Mars gets a bonus point here for urging daily consumption, as per Pringles' permission not to stop.

So, the evidence stacks up. When you're writing a slogan that you want customers to believe in and call to mind at the right moment — for a better line, use a rhyme.

We're all ears

A rhyme sounds pleasing to the ear as our brains can process these phrases smoothly. It's nice and easy. So, the way that things sound really matters — and not just when it comes to words.

With this next behavioral bias, we'll take a slightly different approach from the other chapters in this book. Rather than looking at a bias that Pringles harnessed to power its success, we'll examine how their chips have been used to prove a behavioral science idea. It's worth taking this slight detour as there are lots of ways you can apply the insights from this finding.

When Pringles launched, one of the issues P&G aimed to solve was how to keep the chips whole, unbroken and fresh. The resealable airtight tube facilitates this perfectly. So perfectly, in fact, that Professor Charles Spence at the University of Oxford decided to use Pringles to test a theory about sound.

In 2004, along with colleague Massimiliano Zampini, Spence recruited a group of participants and gave them 180 original flavor Pringles chips and a pair of headphones. They sat down in front of a microphone as they chomped through the chips, and the researchers played the sound back to them through their headphones. The playback volume of the crunch sound was altered — sometimes louder, sometimes quieter. Participants then rated how fresh and tasty the chips were.

All chips in the study were equally fresh, but as the results came in, it became clear that testers experienced something different. It turned out that the louder the volume of the crunch playback, the fresher the crisps seemed. Overall, a loud crunch was associated with 15% more freshness than a quiet one.

The study clearly shows that our perceptions of food freshness are not only dependent on taste; they are also influenced by sound.

This is an example of a phenomenon called *synesthesia* — when stimulation of one sensory pathway (e.g., hearing) also generates a response in another (e.g., taste). In rare cases, this can be quite extreme, so that a person hears a sound or a word and it "tastes" of something even though they are not eating — maybe your professor's voice tastes like potatoes, for example. But in a more subtle and common variation, sound simply influences the flavor of food or drink you are consuming.

Does that sound good?

One demonstration of this sensory overlap comes from Adrian North, then professor of psychology at Heriot-Watt University. In his 1999 study, he offered students a glass of red wine (Cabernet Sauvignon) or white wine (Chardonnay). The wines were tasted as participants listened to various pieces of music, such as Orff's *Carmina Burana*, described as "powerful and heavy;" *Waltz of the Flowers* from *The Nutcracker Suite* by Tchaikovsky — "subtle and refined;" *Just Can't Get Enough* by Nouvelle Vague — "zingy and refreshing;" and *Slow Breakdown* by Michael Brook — a "mellow and soft" tune.

Participants were asked to rate the wines on a scale from 0 to 10 according to these same descriptions (0 = the wine definitely does not have this characteristic; 10 = the wine definitely does have this characteristic).

The results showed that the wines scored consistently highest on the characteristic that matched the music they were listening to when they drank it. For example, when listening to "mellow and soft" music, the wine being tasted would be rated as more "mellow and soft." These characteristics all appeared less dominant when there was no music.

So, it's clear that music can dramatically change our appreciation of flavor. If you work in the hospitality industry, that's something to bear in mind when setting the tone of your eatery. Serving salads?

Better pair them with zingy and refreshing music. Steak and red wine? Maybe something powerful to match.

But it's not just that music can alter taste perception. It has other effects too, which could be significant for any brand with a shop floor. Because multiple studies have found that music influences customers' willingness to pay.

For example, a 2003 study — again by Adrian North — explored the impact of different music types in a high-end restaurant. Over the course of 18 nights, the music that was played in the restaurant changed: some evenings it was classical; others pop; and some nights there was no music.

On examining diners' bills, North discovered that the average spend was £30 per person with no background music. This dropped a little, to £29, when customers dined to pop tunes. But the biggest change was during classical evenings: average spend rose to £33, a statistically significant boost of 10% compared to a quiet atmosphere and 14% more than pop nights.

The most likely explanation is a perceived congruence between classical music and luxury or wealth. And wealthy people spend more, so classical music encourages spending. This is likely to work in other sectors, such as retail or wellness, so it's definitely worth brands considering their playlist carefully.

Worth the weight

There are plenty of other examples of crossover between the senses, where our perceptions in one area influence our experiences in another. Charles Spence describes this in his book *Sensehacking*, and one of the examples he gives — using a Bang & Olufsen remote control to illustrate — is an overlap between the weight of an item and our impression of quality. When you first pick up the remote, you might be surprised at just how heavy it feels. As

Spence observes, this makes it "ooze quality." Interestingly, that was a deliberate move by the brand, which added additional weight beyond the essential electrics. This enhances the perceived depth of the sound we hear from Bang & Olufsen speakers.

A final example comes from a 2015 study led by Charles Michel that examined the effects of cutlery weight on food liking and willingness to pay in a real-world setting.

At a conference in Edinburgh, 121 attendees had been randomly assigned to sit at different tables in an upmarket restaurant. Half the tables were set with lightweight canteen cutlery, while the others were set with heavy, expensive silverware.

Attendees were later asked how much they liked the food on a seven-point scale (one = not at all; seven = very much). They also reported how much they would have been willing to pay for the dish.

The researchers found that those using light cutlery gave an average food rating of 5.1, while those with heavy cutlery rated the same dish as 5.7 — a 12% improvement. And those with lighter utensils were willing to pay an average of £12 for the meal, compared to £13.90 among those using heavy ones — an uplift of 16%.

The researchers suggest that these differences arise because, for most participants, heavy cutlery is distinct from their day-to-day experience. Noticing the weightier cutlery directed their attention toward eating and boosted sensory appreciation of the dish.

These studies illustrate that there may be significant benefits to considering senses beyond the obvious. It's not just about smell when you're selling a perfume. It's not just about the taste of food in a restaurant. There's an idiom that we "eat with our eyes" — but clearly, we eat with our ears and hands too.

Consider all five senses every time. If you wish to convey quality and expense, could you use a weightier bottle, play classical music, or infuse a shop with scent? If you want to signal no-frills, pared-back pricing, lightweight items and pop music might be the right choice. And if you're selling chips, a loud crunch really matters.

Pringles got it right by maintaining large, consistent chip size and optimum freshness, ensuring the same satisfying sound with each and every bite.

THREE KEY TAKEAWAYS

1. **Rhymes boost believability**: Rhymes are easier to process, which means they seem to make sense to us. If you can work a rhyme into a claim, your customers are more likely to take it as fact.

2. **Rhymes boost recall**: Use rhymes for memorable headlines, straplines and slogans. We find it much easier to recall phrases that rhyme, which makes it easier to bring your brand to mind at decision-making moments.

3. **Design for all the senses**: Consider all five senses as part of product development, packaging and marketing. Perceptions in one sense affect our experiences in the others.

CONCLUSION

In 1840s Vienna, it was safer to give birth in your kitchen than in the city's finest hospital.

Close to 12% of mothers died shortly after labor in some wards at the General Hospital — survival odds akin to playing Russian Roulette. Stories abounded of mothers tearfully begging to be allowed to give birth at home instead.

When Ignaz Semmelweis joined the hospital as a young doctor in 1846, he was shocked by such needless suffering, and resolved to act.

One glimmer of hope came from the maternity ward staffed solely by female midwives, where the mortality rate was a fifth of the doctor-led unit.[72]

But to emulate the midwives' ward, Semmelweis first had to unearth what was responsible for the differing outcomes. He conducted a few exploratory tests but they came to nothing.

Eventually, he wondered if the dire survival rates in the doctors' ward could be related to their central role in undertaking autopsies. Sometimes, the doctors would come directly from what they called the "dead house" to the labor ward. Perhaps, thought Semmelweis, "cadaverous particles" were being spread from one to the other, causing infections?

His solution? He suggested the doctors scrub their hands until they could no longer detect the putrid smell of decay. It might seem obvious today — but in an era before germ theory, this was a radical idea.

In 1847, Semmelweis mandated that all doctors entering the maternity wards must wash their hands in a chlorine solution.

The result?

Death rates plummeted.

In the final seven months of 1847, of the 1,841 women who gave birth, just 56 died. That's a fatality rate of 3% — roughly a quarter of the level previously endured by the women of Vienna.[73] It was a medical miracle.

From life to death

But Semmelweis' joy was short-lived.

To his horror, he was unable to persuade other hospitals to follow his recommendations. His advice contradicted received wisdom — to embrace his findings, doctors would have had to accept that their past behavior had caused unnecessary deaths.

Additionally, his message was hampered by the fact that he was relatively low-status. In 1847 he was a 29-year-old doctor who had only been qualified for three years.

To make matters worse, he was averse to publicizing his findings. It would be 11 years before he published *The Etiology of Childbed Fever*, in 1858.

As the stress at his impotence grew, Semmelweis' attacks on the medical establishment became increasingly emotional. He accused them of being "irresponsible murderers." In one desperate attempt at influence, he dumped soiled bedsheets on the desk of a hospital governor.

Eventually, in 1861, his wife — at her wit's end — tricked him

CONCLUSION

into visiting a local asylum, telling him they were going for a daytrip. When Semmelweis arrived he was violently seized by the guards and sectioned.

Unfortunately, he was injured in the struggle and, just two weeks later, he died from an infection from his wound.

Ironically, the cause of death was a general sepsis, the very disease he had tried to eradicate in the maternity wards.

Knowing isn't enough

The theme of Semmelweis' story is not unique. In fact, it's such a common occurrence that the term *Semmelweis reflex* has been coined to describe the tendency for new ideas to be ignored if they challenge established beliefs.

There is no shortage of great medical ideas that failed to take off immediately. Edward Jenner discovered an effective Smallpox vaccination in 1796 but it took dozens of years to become standard practice.

Or, more recently, in 1982 Barry Marshall and Robin Warren uncovered that most stomach ulcers are caused by *H. pylori* — famously, Marshall ingested a culture of the bacteria and then suffered the resulting gastritis. But still, they struggled to persuade others. More than 20 years later, in his Nobel prize acceptance speech, Marshall recounted the medical establishment's initial skepticism: to them "the concept of a germ causing ulcers was like saying the earth is flat."

> New ideas tend to be ignored if they challenge established beliefs.

Discovering the truth and convincing others of that truth are wildly different challenges.

It's not just in the rarefied field of medical discoveries that this happens. The business world is equally culpable. Think about the times you've had an inspired insight but it has fallen on deaf ears. Perhaps at work you've had a brilliant suggestion, yet the client or internal decision-makers have remained unmoved.

Use evidence to influence

Luckily, behavioral science can help.

So far in the book we've discussed how behavioral science studies identify insights that can be put to practical — and profitable — use. But you can also use these experiments to persuade others to adopt your ideas.

Let's say you want to encourage a client to break their category conventions.

Just stressing your authority or experience tends to be ineffective. This confrontational approach can elicit a negative response in the listener. They think to themselves, what about *my* experience or *my* authority? If the other party agrees, it's a tacit admission that they have less relevant experience or authority. Arguments go on and on, round and round. You might try to showcase other brands where similar ideas have been successfully applied… but it's not always enough.

Instead, take them through the Von Restorff experiments: the methodology, the credentials of the academic, the results and the implications. In our 50 years of combined experience, we've never found a more effective route to persuasion.

Presenting the evidence shifts the conversation from *should* we behave distinctively, to *how* do we behave distinctively.

There are three key reasons why the use of behavioral science experiments are so persuasive:

CONCLUSION

1. **Impartiality**: These studies aren't run by commercial providers who profit if you adopt their advice. They're run by researchers interested in seeking the truth. This neutrality makes the studies believable.
2. **Intellectual credibility**: The studies are conducted by researchers at some of the most prestigious universities in the world and reviewed by their peers. This gives them credibility in even the most data-driven organization.
3. **In plain view**: There are no black boxes in these experiments. You're not asking people to take your suggestions on faith. Once you have explained the study, your audience can apply it in the way that feels best. This involvement makes the audience feel engaged.

Of course, sometimes you might have a particularly reticent audience. Maybe they doubt the applicability of the study to their specific category. In that case, try and re-run the experiment for your own brand. Think of the ways you can use your own business, website, or shop as a giant laboratory.

The methodologies for all the studies are in the public domain. Just re-run the studies but adapt them to reflect the market and category you're in. This makes the findings even more indisputable.

Behavioral science has two big benefits. It identifies the truth about what motivates shoppers but crucially it also gives you the ammunition to make your ideas impossible to ignore.

So what are you waiting for?

FURTHER RESOURCES

Hacking the Human Mind Online @ the Consumer Behavior Lab

If you enjoyed this book, there's more. We've built an online hub for *Hacking the Human Mind* at www.theconsumerbehaviorlab.com/HTHM that has live links to the case studies in this book, exclusive content not found in print, and our Hacking the Human Mind Masterclass — designed to help you take the concepts in *Hacking the Human Mind* and put them into action inside your company. Using the hub's short, practical learning modules, you can learn directly from us and hear more examples that didn't make it into the book.

The Consumer Behavior Lab (CBL) is our broader initiative dedicated to teaching marketers how to apply behavioral science. At CBL, we collaborate with brands around the globe to turn academic research into commercial impact.

The Behavioral Science for Brands podcast

Our podcast (www.BSci4Brands.com) looks at the behavioral science secrets of some of the world's best brands. Each episode is 20 to 40 minutes long and covers one or two of the psychological principles that the brand in question has used to fuel its success.

If that approach sounds familiar, it's no coincidence — the idea for *Hacking the Human Mind* came during a recording of the podcast. The show casts a wider net than the book, covering brands from L'Oréal to Grey Goose, Chipotle to Costco. It's a great companion resource if you want to keep learning on the go, and it continues to evolve as we explore new campaigns, case studies, and fresh insights from behavioral science.

The Choice Factory: 25 Behavioural Biases That Influence What We Buy by Richard Shotton [2018]
The Illusion of Choice: 16½ Psychological Biases That Influence What We Buy by Richard Shotton [2023]

If you enjoyed *Hacking the Human Mind* then Richard has written two other books on applying behavioral science to marketing. In *The Choice Factory* he identified 25 biases that marketers can harness to improve their marketing. Five years later he released the follow-up, *The Illusion of Choice*, in which he identified another 16½ insights. (The ½ chapter is a short section on why people tend to believe precise numbers more than suspiciously round ones.)

Messengers: Who We Listen To, Who We Don't, and Why by Steve Martin and Joseph Marks [2019]

Steve Martin is perhaps best known as a long-time collaborator with Robert Cialdini, one of the most influential academics in the field. The two have co-authored books such as *Yes!* and *The Small Big*.

However, for this book, Martin has partnered with Joseph Marks, a researcher at UCL, to take an in-depth look at the messenger effect. This is the finding that the persuasive power of a message varies according to who delivered it. We covered this bias in the Got Milk? chapter.

Hit Makers: How to Succeed in an Age of Distraction by Derek Thompson [2017]

Derek Thompson, a staff writer at *The Atlantic*, investigates why some products flop and others become hits. In his wide-ranging book, he covers the secrets behind hits from *Fifty Shades of Grey* to Brahm's lullaby; Instagram to Star Wars.

One of the ideas covered is MAYA — Raymond Loewy's principle of most advanced yet acceptable. We featured this in the Apple chapter so if you enjoyed that, you can find out more with this book.

The Expectation Effect: How Your Mindset Can Change Your World by David Robson [2022]

The Expectation Effect was picked by the *Financial Times* as their best health and well-being book of 2022. It's written by David Robson, a senior journalist at *BBC Future* who has a gift for communicating complex ideas in simple terms. In this book he investigates how our prior expectations affect our actual experience. We discussed this insight in the chapter on Kraft mac & cheese but Robson's book goes into far more detail.

Writing for Busy Readers: Communicate More Effectively in the Real World by Todd Rogers and Jessica Lasky-Fink [2023]

There is a long history of books on how to write more effectively. The classic in the genre, Strunk and White's *The Elements of Style*, was published way back in 1959. However, Todd Rogers and Jessica Lasky-Fink, two behavioral scientists at Harvard University, take a fresh approach. Rather than speculate about what makes for clear and effective communications they look at the experimental evidence. The recommendations they make are highly practical.

Sense Hacking: How to Use the Power of Your Senses for Happier, Healthier Living by Charles Spence [2021]

Charles Spence, a professor at Oxford University, is interested in cross-modal correspondence. This is the finding that our senses are interconnected to a surprising degree, so that, say, what we taste is deeply affected by what it sounds, feels, or looks like. His research focuses on how chefs, restaurants, and food brands can use these insights. We covered some of that work in the Pringles chapter.

Sense Hacking isn't Spence's only book, but it's his most broad-ranging and the findings extend beyond the kitchen. If you're specifically interested in the applications for food, check out the more focused *Gastrophysics* and *The Perfect Meal*.

Handbook on the Psychology of Pricing: 100+ Effects on Persuasion and Influence Every Entrepreneur, Marketer, and Pricing Manager Needs to Know by Dr. Markus Husemann-Kopetzky [2018]

The psychology of pricing is a fascinating area of research. While there are lots of good books on the topic this handbook is probably the most comprehensive. In the *Psychology of Pricing*, Markus Husemann-Kopetzky provides short digests of hundreds of experiments. Unlike the other books on the list, this isn't one to sit down and read in successive sittings but better to keep it handy on your desk for any time a pricing query arises.

How Not to Plan: 66 Ways to Screw it Up by Les Binet and Sarah Carter [2018]

In this book Les Binet and Sarah Carter bust a series of myths that afflict marketing. They cover everything from how to set objectives, the 4 Ps, research and analysis, to briefing, creative work, and media and effectiveness.

It's not about behavioral science per se but they regularly draw on principles from the field to explain what works and what doesn't.

The format of the book — it's broken into 66 short chapters — means it's super easy to get through.

REFERENCES

Introduction

Zhang, Ying, Ayelet Fishbach and Arie W. Kruglanski, "The Dilution Model: How Additional Goals Undermine the Perceived Instrumentality of a Shared Path," *Journal of Personality and Social Psychology*, 92(3), 389-401, 2007.

Chapter 1: Kraft Mac & Cheese

Guido, Gianluigi, Marco Pichierri, Giovanni Pino and Rajan Nataraajan, "Effects of Face Images and Face Pareidolia on Consumers' Responses to Print Advertising: An Empirical Investigation," *Journal of Advertising Research*, 59(2), 219–231, 2019.

Lee, Leonard, Shane Frederick and Dan Ariely, "Try It, You'll Like It: The Influence of Expectation, Consumption, and Revelation on Preferences for Beer," *Psychological Science*, 17(12), 1054–1058, 2006.

Raghunathan, Rajagopal, Rebecca Walker Naylor and Wayne D. Hoyer, "The Unhealthy = Tasty Intuition and Its Effects on Taste Inferences, Enjoyment, and Choice of Food Products," *Journal of Marketing*, 70(4), 170–184, 2006.

Read, Daniel and Barbara van Leeuwen, "Predicting Hunger: The Effects of Appetite and Delay on Choice," *Organizational Behavior and Human Decision Processes*, 76(2), 189–205, 1998.

Robson, David "Neuroscience: Why Do We See Faces in Everyday Objects?" *BBC News*, 2014.

Turnwald, Bradley P., Danielle Z. Boles and Alia J. Crum, "Association Between Indulgent Descriptions and Vegetable Consumption: Twisted Carrots and Dynamite Beets," *JAMA Internal Medicine*, 177(8), 1216–1218, 2017.

Chapter 2: Starbucks' Pumpkin Spice Latte

Lasaleta, Jannine D., Constantine Sedikides and Kathleen D. Vohs, "Nostalgia Weakens the Desire for Money," *Journal of Consumer Research*, 41(3), 713–729, 2014.

Lee, Seung Yun and Russell Seidle, "Narcissists as Consumers: The Effects of Perceived Scarcity on Processing of Product Information," *Social Behavior and Personality*, 40(9), 1485–1499, 2012.

Sharot, Tali, and Cass R. Sunstein, *Look Again: The Power of Noticing What Was Always There*. Atria/One Signal Publishers. 2025.

Nelson, Leif D. and Tom Meyvis, "Interrupted Consumption: Disrupting Adaptation to Hedonic Experiences," *Journal of Marketing Research*, 45(6), 654–664, 2008.

Shu, Suzanne B. and Ayelet Gneezy, "Procrastination of Enjoyable Experiences," *Journal of Marketing Research*, 47(5), 933–944, 2010.

Chapter 3: Snickers

Gollwitzer, Peter M. and Veronika Brandstätter, "Implementation Intentions and Effective Goal Pursuit," *Journal of Personality and Social Psychology*, 73(1), 186–199, 1997.

Milne, Sarah, Sheina Orbell and Paschal Sheeran, "Combining Motivational and Volitional Interventions to Promote Exercise Participation: Protection Motivation Theory and Implementation Intentions," *British Journal of Health Psychology*, 7(2), 163–184, 2002.

Eisend, Martin, "A Meta-analysis of Humor in Advertising," *Journal of the Academy of Marketing Science*, 37, 191–203, 2009.

Boyd, Dom, Ecem Erdem and Polly Wyn Jones, "Time to Get Serious About Humour in Advertising," Kantar, August 15, 2024. www.kantar.com/inspiration/advertising-media/time-to-get-serious-about-humour-in-advertising.

Nerhardt, Göran, "Humor and Inclination to Laugh: Emotional Reactions to Stimuli of Different Divergence from a Range of Expectancy," *Scandinavian Journal of Psychology*, 11(1), 185–195, 1970.

REFERENCES

Chapter 4: Apple

Begg, Ian, "Recall of Meaningful Phrases," *Journal of Verbal Learning and Verbal Behaviour*, 11(4), 431–439, 1972.

Boudreau, Kevin, Eva Guinan, Karim Lakhani and Christoph Riedl, "The Novelty Paradox and Bias for Normal Science: Evidence from Randomized Medical Grant Proposal Evaluations," *Harvard Business School Working Paper*, No. 13–53, 2012.

Hargadon, Andrew and Yellowlees Douglas, "When Innovations Meet Institutions: Edison and the Design of the Electric Light," *Administrative Science Quarterly*, 46(3), 476–450, 2001.

Hekkert, Paul, Dirk Snelders and Piet C. van Wieringen, "'Most Advanced, Yet Acceptable': Typicality and Novelty as Joint Predictors of Aesthetic Preference in Industrial Design," *British Journal of Psychology*, 94, 111–124, 2003.

Thompson, Derek, "The Four Letter Code to Selling Just About Anything," *The Atlantic*, 2017.

Thompson, Derek, *Hit Makers: How Things Become Popular*. Penguin. 2017

Uzzi, Brian, Satyam Mukherjee, Michael Stringer and Ben Jones, "Atypical Combinations and Scientific Impact," *Science*, 342(6157), 468–472, 2013.

Wood, Orlando, *Lemon. How the Advertising Brain Turned Sour*. IPA. 2019.

Chapter 5: Amazon Prime

Arkes, Hal R. and Catherine Blumer, "The Psychology of Sunk Cost," *Organizational Behavior and Human Decision Processes*, 35(1), 124–140, 1985.

Gourville, John T. and Dilip Soman, "Payment Depreciation: The Behavioral Effects of Temporally Separating Payments from Consumption," *Journal of Consumer Research*, 25(2), 160–174, 1998.

Kivetz, Ran, Oleg Urminsky and Yuhuang Zheng, "The Goal-Gradient Hypothesis Resurrected: Purchase Acceleration, Illusionary Goal Progress, and Customer Retention," *Journal of Marketing Research*, 43(1), 39–58, 2006.

Roth, Stefan, Thomas Robbert and Lennart Straus, "On the Sunk-Cost Effect in Economic Decision-Making: A Meta-analytic Review," *Business Research*, 8, 99–138, 2015.

Strulov-Shlain, Avner, "More than a Penny's Worth: Left-Digit Bias and Firm Pricing," *Review of Economic Studies*, 90(5), 2612–2645, 2023.

Chapter 6: Aperol

The Behavioural Insights Team, Applying behavioural insights to reduce fraud, error and debt. Cabinet Office. 2012.

Cialdini, Robert, *Influence: Science and Practice*. Pearson. 1984.

Keizer, Kees, Siegwart Lindenberg and Linda Steg, "The Spreading of Disorder," *Science*, 322, 1681–1685, 2008.

Berger, Jonah, *Contagious: Why Things Catch On*. Simon & Schuster. 2013.

Peterson, Robert, Yeolib Kim and Jaeseok Jeong, "Out-of-Stock, Sold Out, or Unavailable? Framing a Product Outage in Online Retailing," *Marketing Letters*, 37(3), 428–440, 2019.

Breeze, James, "Here's Looking at You!" *LinkedIn*, August 13, 2014.

Chapter 7: Häagen-Dazs

Nathan, Joan, "Ice Cream's Jewish Innovators," *Tablet Magazine*, August 2, 2012.

Carlson, Michael, "Rose Mattus," *The Guardian*, January 9, 2007.

Wansink, Brian, Colin Payne and Jill North, "Fine as North Dakota Wine," *Physiological Behaviour*, 90(5), 712–716, 2007.

Akdeniz Ar, Aybeniz and Ali Kara, "Emerging Market Consumers' Country of Production Image, Trust and Quality Perceptions of Global Brands Made-in China," *Journal of Product & Brand Management*, 23(7), 491–503, 2014.

Aichner, Thomas, Cipriano Forza and Alessio Trentin, "The Country-of-Origin Lie: Impact of Foreign Branding on Customers' Willingness to Buy and Willingness to Pay When the Product's Actual Origin is Disclosed," *The International Review of Retail, Distribution and Consumer Research*, 27(1), 43–60, 2017.

Blumenthal, Karen, *Grande Expectations: A Year in the Life of Starbucks' Stock*. Crown Business. 2007.

Thaler, Richard H. and Cass R. Sunstein, *Nudge: Improving Decisions about Health, Wealth and Happiness*. Penguin Books. 2009.

REFERENCES

Nosowitz, Dan, "Häagen-Dazs Ice Cream Is From the Bronx — So What's With the Name?" *Atlas Obscura*, September 5, 2017.

Loftus, Elizabeth and John Palmer, "Reconstruction of Automobile Destruction: An Example of the Interaction between Language and Memory," *Journal of Verbal Learning & Verbal Behavior*, 13(5), 585–589, 1974.

Luntz, Frank, *Words That Work: It's Not What You Say, It's What People Hear*. Grand Central Publishing. 2008.

Chapter 8: Red Bull

Kirmani, Anna and Peter Wright, "Money Talks: Perceived Advertising Expense and Expected Product Quality," *Journal of Consumer Research*, 16(3), 344–353, 1989.

Plassmann, Hilke, John O'Doherty, Baba Shiv and Antonio Rangel, "Marketing Actions Can Modulate Neural Representations of Experienced Pleasantness," Proceedings of the National Academy of Sciences of the United States of America, 105(3), 1050–1054, 2008.

Just, David R., Özge Sığırcı and Brian Wansink, "Lower Buffet Prices Lead to Less Taste Satisfaction," *Journal of Sensory Studies*, 29(5), 362–370, 2014.

Sutherland, Rory, *Alchemy*. WH Allen. 2019.

Thinkbox, *Signalling Success*. Thinkbox. 2020.

Chapter 9: Guinness

Aronson, Elliot, Ben Willerman and Joanne Floyd, "The Effect of a Pratfall on Increasing Interpersonal Attractiveness," *Psychonomic Science*, 4(6), 227–228, 1966.

Bohner, Gerd, Sabine Einwiller, Hans-Peter Erb and Frank Siebler. "When Small Means Comfortable: Relations Between Product Attributes in Two-sided Advertising." *Journal of Consumer Psychology*, 13(4), 454–463, 2003.

Williams, Kipling D., Martin J. Bourgeois and Robert T. Croyle, "The Effects of Stealing Thunder in Criminal and Civil Trials," *Law and Human Behavior*, 7(6), 597–609, 1993.

Chapter 10: Liquid Death

Australian Department of Health "Nudge vs Superbugs," 2018.

von Restorff, Hedwig, "On the Effect of Area Formation in the Trace Field," *Psychologische Forschung*, 18(1), 299–342, 1933.

Zappi, *The State of Creative Effectiveness*. Zappi. 2023.

Zajonc, Robert, "Attitudinal Effects of Mere Exposure," *Journal of Personality and Social Psychology*, 9(2), 1–27, 1968.

Chapter 11: Dyson

Buell, Ryan W., Tami Kim and Chia-Jung Tsay, "Creating Reciprocal Value through Operational Transparency," *Management Science*, 63(6), 1673–1695, 2015.

Buell, Ryan W. and Michael I. Norton, "The Labor Illusion: How Operational Transparency Increases Perceived Value," *Management Science*, 57(9), 1564–1579, 2011.

Kruger, Justin, Derrick Wirtz, Leaf Van Boven and T. William Altermatt, "The Effort Heuristic," *Journal of Experimental Social Psychology*, 40(1), 91–98, 2004.

Millet, Kobe, Florian Buehler, Guanzhong Du and Michail D. Kokkoris, "Defending Humankind: Anthropocentric Bias in the Appreciation of AI Art," *Computers in Human Behavior*, 143, 107707, 2023.

Chapter 12: Facebook

Alter, Adam, *Irresistible*. Bodley Head. 2017.

Corrigan, Jay, Saleem Alhabash, Matthew Rousu and Sean Cash, "How Much is Social Media Worth? Estimating the Value of Facebook by Paying Users to Stop Using It," *PLoS One*, 13(12), e0207101, 2018.

Geier, Andrew, Brian Wansink and Paul Rozin, "Red Potato Chips: Segmentation Cues Can Substantially Decrease Food Intake," *Health Psychology*, 31(3), 398–401, 2012.

Gneezy, Uri. *Mixed Signals: How Incentives Really Work*. Yale University Press. 2023.

Mazar, Nina, Kristina Shampanier and Dan Ariely, "When Retailing and Las

Vegas Meet: Probabilistic Free Price Promotions," *Management Science*, 63(1), 250–266, 2017.

Wadhwa, Monica and JeeHye Christine Kim, "Can a Near Win Kindle Motivation? The Impact of Nearly Winning on Motivation for Unrelated Rewards," *Psychological Science*, 26(6), 701–708, 2015.

Zeelenberg, Marcel and Rik Pieters, "Consequences of Regret Aversion in Real Life: The Case of the Dutch Postcode Lottery," *Organizational Behavior and Human Decision Processes*, 93(2), 155–168, 2004.

Zeiler, Michael, "Fixed-Interval Behaviour: Effects of Percentage Reinforcement," *Journal of the Experimental Analysis of Behaviour*, 17(2), 177–189, 1972.

Chapter 13: Klarna

Breman, Anna, "Give More Tomorrow: Two Field Experiments on Altruism and Intertemporal Choice," *Journal of Public Economics*, 95(11–12), 1349–1357, 2011.

Delaney, Liam and Leonhard K. Lades "Present Bias and Everyday Self-Control Failures: A Day Reconstruction Study," *Journal of Behavioural Decision Making*, 30(5), 1157–1167, 2017.

Gourville, John T., "Pennies-a-Day: The Effect of Temporal Reframing on Transaction Evaluation," *Journal of Consumer Research*, 24(4), 395–408, 1998.

O'Hear, Steve, "Making Sense of Klarna," *TechCrunch*, December 8, 2020. techcrunch.com/2020/12/08/making-sense-of-klarna/

Chapter 14: Got Milk?

Daddona, Matthew, "Got Milk? How the Iconic Campaign Came to Be, 25 Years Ago," *Fast Company*, June 13, 2018. www.fastcompany.com/40556502/got-milk-how-the-iconic-campaign-came-to-be-25-years-ago

Gonzales, Marti Hope, Elliot Aronson and Mark A. Costanzo, "Using Social Cognition and Persuasion to Promote Energy Conservation: A Quasi-Experiment," *Journal of Applied Social Psychology*, 18(12), 1049–1066, 1988.

Hovland, Carl I. and Walter Weiss, "The Influence of Source Credibility on Communication Effectiveness," *Public Opinion Quarterly*, 15(4), 635–650, 1951.

Javdani, Mohsen and Ha-Joon Chang, "Who Said or What Said? Estimating Ideological Bias in Views among Economists," *Cambridge Journal of Economics*, 47(2), 309–339, 2023.

Kahneman, Daniel and Amos Tversky, "Prospect Theory: An Analysis of Decision under Risk," *Econometrica*, 47, 263–291, 1979.

Knoll, Johannes and Jörg Matthes, "The Effectiveness of Celebrity Endorsements: A Meta-analysis," *Journal of the Academy of Marketing Science*, 45, 55–75, 2017.

Steel, Jon, *Truth, Lies, and Advertising: The Art of Account Planning*. John Wiley & Sons. 1998.

Chapter 15: Kentucky Fried Chicken

Blaess, Nine, "How Ogilvy Used Psychology to Increase Sales of KFC French Fries by 56%," *Brie Stewart*, n.d.

Browne, Will and Mike Swarbrick Jones, "What Works in E-commerce – a Meta-analysis of 6700 Online Experiments," *Qubit Digital Ltd*, 21, 2017.

Heimbach, James T. and Jacob Jacoby, "The Zeigarnik Effect in Advertising," *Association for Consumer Research (3rd Annual Conference)*, 746–757, 1972.

Lee, Seung Yun and Russell Seidle, "Narcissists as Consumers: The Effects of Perceived Scarcity on Processing of Product Information," *Social Behavior and Personality*, 40(9), 1485–1499, 2012.

Lehrer, Jonah, "The Itch of Curiosity," *WIRED*, August 3, 2010. www.wired.com/2010/08/the-itch-of-curiosity/

Loewenstein, George, "The Psychology of Curiosity: A Review and Reinterpretation," *Psychological Bulletin*, 116(1), 75, 1994.

Moraza, Nathan, "KFC's Secret Menu," *Nathan Moraza*, 2020.

Stewart, Brie, "90 Ways to Say $1 Chips," *Brie Stewart*, 2018.

Wansink, Brian, Robert J. Kent and Stephen J. Hoch, "An Anchoring and Adjustment Model of Purchase Quantity Decisions," *Journal of Marketing Research*, 35(1), 71–81, 1998.

Zeigarnik, Bluma, "On Finished and Unfinished Tasks," *Psychologische Forschungen*, 9, 1–85, 1927.

REFERENCES

Chapter 16: Pringles

Filkuková, Petra and Sven Hroar Klempe, "Rhyme as Reason in Commercial and Social Advertising," *Scandinavian Journal of Psychology*, 54(5), 423–431, 2013.

McGlone, Matthew S. and Jessica Tofighbakhsh, "The Keats Heuristic: Rhyme as Reason in Aphorism Interpretation," *Poetics*, 26(4), 235–244, 1999.

Michel, Charles, Carlos Velasco and Charles Spence, "Cutlery Matters: Heavy Cutlery Enhances Diners' Enjoyment of the Food Served in a Realistic Dining Environment," *Flavour*, 4(26), 1–8, 2015.

North, Adrian C., "The Effect of Background Music on the Taste of Wine," *British Journal of Psychology*, 103(3), 293–301, 2012.

North, Adrian C., Amber Shilcock and David J. Hargreaves, "The Effect of Musical Style on Restaurant Customers' Spending," *Environment and Behavior*, 35(5), 712–718, 2003.

Spence, Charles, *Sense-hacking: How to Use the Power of Your Senses for Happier, Healthier Living*. Penguin. 2022.

Zampini, Massimiliano and Charles Spence, "The Role of Auditory Cues in Modulating the Perceived Crispness and Staleness of Potato Chips," *Journal of Sensory Studies*, 19(5), 347–363, 2004.

ENDNOTES

1. Podcast: How I built this with Guy Raz. Five Guys: Jerry Murrell.
2. www.fiveguys.com/-/media/public-site/files/media-fact-sheets/five-guys-media-fact-sheet-web.pdf.
3. www.americanbuildersquarterly.com/2024/five-guys-stands-apart-from-the-competition.
4. www.restaurantbusinessonline.com/top-500-chains-2024/five-guys.
5. www.huffpost.com/entry/10-things-you-didnt-know_b_6327382.
6. www.news.kraftheinzcompany.com/press-releases-details/2022.
7. www.kaylin-goldstein.com/works/worlds-largest-blind-taste-test.
8. www.britannica.com/money/Starbucks.
9. www.forbes.com/sites/michelinemaynard/2013/09/22/how-starbucks-turned-pumpkin-spice-into-a-marketing-bonanza.
10. www.snickers.com/our-story.
11. www.yahoo.com/lifestyle/most-popular-candy-bar-us-184555355.html.
12. www.medium.com/better-marketing.
13. www.landingi.com/social-media-marketing/traditional-marketing-compared.
14. www.apple.com/newsroom/2024/02/apple-reports-first-quarter-results.
15. www.statista.com/topics/846/amazon; www.marketwatch.com/story/heres-why-a-whopping-83-of-american-households-now-shop-at-amazon.
16. www.statista.com/topics/4076/amazon-prime/#topicOverview.
17. www.explodingtopics.com/blog/amazon-prime-member-stats.
18. Gabrielle Olya, "How Does Your Amazon Spending Compare to the Average American's?", *Yahoo! Finance*, July 18, 2023.

19 www.tabletmag.com/sections/food/articles/ice-creams-jewish-innovators.

20 www.tabletmag.com/sections/food/articles/ice-creams-jewish-innovators.

21 www.nytimes.com/2006/12/01/obituaries/01mattus.html.

22 It's worth noting that some experiments by Wansink have since been retracted. However, this study is not one of them. You can check which papers have been retracted here: retractiondatabase.org/RetractionSearch.aspx.

23 If you're curious about Starbucks sizes, some light is shed on this in Brooke Nelson Alexander, "Want to Know About Starbucks Cup Sizes," *Reader's Digest*, September 1, 2023.

24 patagonian-toothfish-story.msc.org.

25 www.redbull.com/gb-en/energydrink/company-profile.

26 Declaration of interest: Richard advised Thinkbox regarding behavioral science during the early parts of their study.

27 www.economist.com/business/2002/05/09/selling-energy.

28 www.pbs.org/newshour/nation/full-length-video-of-felix-baumgartners-242-mile-jump-released-on-first-anniversary.

29 www.redbull.com/gb-en/best-of-2012-red-bull-stratos.

30 www.thetimes.com/sunday-times-100-tech/hardware-profile/article.

31 ww.medium.com/better-marketing/red-bulls-30-million-marketing-stunt-almost-didn-t-happen-88d24fefdeff.

32 www.diageo.com/en/news-and-media/press-releases/2025/guinness-us-spotlights-lovely-days-across-the-country-in-new-campaign.

33 www.guinnesscelebrate.com/download/03-01_The_Quality_Chain_Full_Presentation.pdf.

34 Guinness, "Swim Black." www.youtu.be/EZbMSCuGl3k?si=CjtYoTwEVXTnSVZa.

35 Guinness, "Surfer." www.youtu.be/w9ogzVyTtcw?si=smVnHUHowvDeoK_R.

36 www.marketingweek.com/guinness-surfer/.

37 Guinness and Joe Montana, www.youtu.be/dUI-iZnUOaA?si=M72Kv_KerGV8iDv5.

ENDNOTES

38 www.forbes.com/sites/tomward/2022/11/23/mike-cessario-is-a-marketing-genius.

39 www.cnbc.com/2022/11/26/liquid-death-ceo-mike-cessario-we-chose-the-dumbest-possible-name-for-water.html.

40 www.thegrocer.co.uk/analysis-and-features/what-is-liquid-death-and-is-it-about-to-take-the-uk-by-storm/682693.article.

41 www.time.com/7023597/mike-cessario.

42 www.forbes.com/profile/james-dyson.

43 Stephen Dowling, "Frustration and failure fuel Dyson's success," BBC Future, March 14, 2013, www.bbc.com/future/article/20130312-failure-is-the-best-medicine.

44 www.nedwin.medium.com/the-1-5m-napkin-abd2702927do.

45 Thomas Barrie, "Sir James Dyson: 'Most focus groups are wrong,'" *GQ*, December 1, 2021.

46 www.thecrimson.com/article/2003/11/19.

47 www.loki.editorial.aetnd.com/this-day-in-history/facebook-launches-mark-zuckerberg.

48 www.edition.cnn.com/2014/02/11/world/facebook-fast-facts/index.html.

49 www.statista.com/chart/5380/facebook-user-engagement.

50 www.bbc.co.uk/news/business-18105608.

51 www.uk.finance.yahoo.com/quote/META/?p=FB.

52 www.forbes.com/profile/mark-zuckerberg.

53 www.abcnews.go.com/Business/PersonalFinance/story?id=3771803&page=1.

54 www.chiefmarketer.com/red-sox-win-would-be-furniture-buyers-boon.

55 www.postcodelotterygroup.com/what-we-do/nationale-postcode-loterij.

56 www.klarna.com/international/about-us.

57 www. investors.klarna.com/overview/default.aspx.

58 www.ft.com/content/eaeb36f1-495d-48a1-9d2a-eef87d144670.

59 www.bain.com/insights/assessing-benefits-and-challenges-bnpl-report-2021.

60 www.aef.com/classroom-resources/case-histories/got-milk.

61 www.aef.com/classroom-resources/case-histories/got-milk.

62 Jon Steel, *Truth, Lies, and Advertising: The Art of Account Planning*. John Wiley & Sons. 1998.

63 Matthew Daddona, "Got Milk? How the iconic campaign came to be, 25 years ago," *Fast Company*, June 13, 2018, www.fastcompany.com/40556502/got-milk-how-the-iconic-campaign-came-to-be-25-years-ago.

64 www.c-suitenetwork.com/articles/the-multi-billion-dollar-kfc-franchise-started-as-a-gas-station-recipe.

65 www.global.kfc.com/press-releases/kfc-surpasses-30-000-restaurants-worldwide.

66 www.franchiseeurope.com/top-500/kfc/9.

67 www.nathanmoraza.work/KFC-Secret-Menu.

68 Some experiments by Wansink, especially later ones, have since been retracted. However, this study is not one of them. You can check which papers have been retracted here: www.retractiondatabase.org/RetractionSearch.aspx.

69 www.nineblaess.de/blog/how-ogilvy-used-psychology-to-increase-sales-of-kfc-french-fries-by-56.

70 www.finance.yahoo.com/news/15-biggest-potato-chip-brands-155245264.html.

71 www.finance.yahoo.com/news/why-kellanova-sees-pringles-gateway-105200952.html.

72 www.npr.org/sections/health-shots/2015/01/12/375663920/the-doctor-who-championed-hand-washing-and-saved-women-s-lives.

73 www.wellcomecollection.org/stories/the-father-of-handwashing.

ACKNOWLEDGMENTS

We'd like to thank the dozens of folks — thought leaders in the marketing industry and behavioral science academics — who have partnered with the Consumer Behavior Lab and been featured on our podcast, Behavioral Science for Brands. Many people have provided help with the writing and research of the book. In terms of editing, Craig Pearce and Amy Webber have provided much-needed support.

Walter Campbell, Andy Pearson and Jon Steel kindly gave their first-hand insight for our commentary on Guinness, Liquid Death and the California Milk Processor Board.

The research that was carried out, either specifically for this book or earlier projects, involved input from many people. In particular, Nicki Morley, Jon Puleston, Max Wiggins, Duncan Willett, Sumran Kaul and Mike Treharne.

From Richard

Over the last five years, my work applying behavioral science to marketing has been a joint enterprise. I've been massively helped by Joanna Stanley and Alex Myroshnychenko. Both of whom have worked tirelessly to identify and analyse the most important studies.

General inspiration has — as ever — come from Dave Trott, Rory Sutherland and Robert Cialdini.

Jane McQueen has helped on every book I've worked on but on

Hacking the Human Mind she has been more central than ever — from stylistic decisions to the matters of utmost substance, her role has been invaluable.

Finally, Anna and Tom who have provided much needed encouragement and patiently put up with me trying to turn the studies covered into life lessons.

And, hopefully, now the book is finished they will tap up their school and university libraries to buy a few copies.

From MichaelAaron

To the hundreds of clients who've trusted me with some of their biggest business challenges since I first started at 14 — thank you. To my colleagues and staff — thank you for your collaboration, and belief, in our work.

Particularly deep thanks go to two extraordinary individuals: Pat Donohue and Tim Williams. You are both invaluable advisors and thought partners — helping me become a better person and leader.

I'm deeply thankful to George Rubsam, who opened my eyes (and brain) to the world of marketing. To Tim Frank, who introduced me to the field of behavioral science. And to Frank Salerno, who taught me so much about the beauty — and power — of the written word.

Most of all, I'm especially grateful to my wife, Erika — my fiercest supporter, deepest collaborator, and partner I love sharing every day with. To my parents and brothers, who shaped me in countless positive ways and continue to be sources of inspiration. And to Max, Nina, and Amelia — who are the most important *why* for everything I do.

ABOUT THE AUTHORS

Richard Shotton

Richard Shotton specialises in applying behavioural science to marketing. He is the founder of Astroten, a consultancy that helps brands such as Google, Mondelez and Meta with their challenges.

He is the author of *The Choice Factory* and *The Illusion of Choice*. Two best-selling books, available in 15 languages, which explain how behavioural science can solve business challenges.

In 2021 he became an associate of the Moller Institute, Churchill College, Cambridge University and an honorary fellow of the IPA.

MichaelAaron Flicker

MichaelAaron Flicker is an American entrepreneur who builds companies powered by behavioral science. He is founder and CEO of XenoPsi Ventures, a brand incubator firm that owns, operates and invests in over a dozen companies.

A regular partner to CEOs and their executive teams, he applies behavioral science to unlock brand value and accelerate growth. He is also a regular contributor to Fast Company and other leading industry publications.

MichaelAaron is the founder of the Consumer Behavior Lab (consumerbehaviorlab.com), an initiative dedicated to advancing the marketing industry through evidence-based insights. Named one of NJBIZ's "40 Under 40," his companies have been recognized for three consecutive years on the Inc. 5000 list of America's fastest-growing private businesses.